# *Belgian chocolate*

## pralines, batons, desserts, biscuits ...

## The Author
### Jacques Mercier

RTBF Producer and creator of the famous *Jeu des dictionnaires*. His many works include a fine book on chocolate published by Glénat in 1989.

with **Martine Riboux**.

•

## Production
Christine Kremer and
Valérie Constant: editorial.
Martine Riboux: checking and index.
Élisabeth Gautier: typographical supervision.
Jean-Christophe Bousmar: design.
Helen McPhail: English translation.

•

## Acknowledgements
*Femmes d'Aujourd'hui.*
Institut national des statistiques.
Les producteurs belges de chocolat, de desserts,
de biscuits chocolatés et de pralines.

Jacques Mercier - Preface by Pierre Wynants

# *Belgian chocolate*

## pralines, batons, desserts, biscuits ...

*with recipes
and a guide to the best addresses*

*"Saveurs Gourmandes"*
LA RENAISSANCE DU LIVRE

# Contents

# Contents

# The Charms of E

In their childhood, when my two daughters began to read and understand things, they wondered why newspapers mentioned their parents but never the two girls themselves. For a press lunch some time after that comment I created a dessert with black and white chocolate which I named "gâteau aux chocolats Laurence et Véronique"... And so of course the journalists had to mention the girls too!

Meanwhile Laurence, together with her chef husband Lionel, was already helping her parents in the restaurant. After her training at the Lausanne catering school Véronique took a management course in the United States. Now history has repeated itself once more for the birth of Laurence's daughter, with the creation of a new summer dessert: "Effeuillée aux fruits rouge et chocolat blanc pour Jessica",

# elgian Chocolate !

consisting of very delicate flakes of white chocolate built up like a house of cards with soft fruit.

All through my childhood, chocolate was an important feature: bread and chocolate, Easter eggs, the lovely smell of sweet-shops. I was already living at No. 23, Place Rouppe - I have lived over the restaurant for forty years! - and I went to school at the junction of the Rue du Poinçon and the Rue d'Accolay. I became part of restaurant life at a very young age: when I was three I helped my grandmother with the washing-up - or at least I pretended to help her! Later, my parents, who never stopped working, boarded me out at the Athénée Royal at Soignies. That was when I used to collect the prints of sporting heroes in the wrappers of "Jacques" chocolate bâtons. I was already a fan of Anderlecht Sporting Club: this was the time of

Meert, Decoster, Vaillant, Decorte, Van Steen, Jeng and Hyppolite Vandenbosch, Valet, etc., and above all the centre-forward Joseph Mermans!

I have always championed anything which contributes to our country's fame: our artists - the decor at "Comme Chez Soi" takes its inspiration from Art Nouveau and Victor Horta - and our raw materials, including the chocolate that I use in my creations. This is the Callebaut 90 per cent dark chocolate. My dessert menu (a third of the desserts contain chocolate) always includes gâteaux and ice-creams: there is "Trinitarios", "Chocolate Log with morello cherries", "Brazilian tower" with caramel, and toasted almonds and hazelnuts, and "White Lady in Caribbean costume" consisting of vanilla ice-cream whipped at the last moment with fine-spun caramel, chocolate sauce, and surrounded by banana mousse. Alternatively, there is a hot chocolate soufflé, a creamy warm chocolate cake, or a hot purée of cherries and pineapple with Black Forest cream (a kind of Irish coffee) ...

Eating chocolate continues to be a tremendous pleasure. I sometimes enjoy couverture chocolate (70 per cent pure cocoa) which I cut up into small squares. Sometimes at weekends, I even take a little bit of chocolate home to eat in the evening.

I am delighted when, at the far ends of the earth, I discover "Belgian chocolate", and I am proud of it. I also buy pralines regularly ... In Brussels we are spoilt for choice: the city is well filled with excellent chocolate shops!

At first, cooking was my hobby, then it became a passion and I made it my profession. I try to give my guests as much pleasure as possible, and my chefs the art of communication and passing on our traditions.

Pierre Wynants

"Comme Chez Soi", 23 place Rouppe, 1000 Brussels.
(Tel. : 02/512.29.21).
The restaurant opened in 1926. Marie-Thérèse and Pierre Wynants are the third generation of the family, Laurence and Lionel will be the fourth. All gastronomy guides heap praise upon it, and their highest recommendations: (in alphabetical order) Le Bottin Gourmand, Le Champerard, Delta, Gault et Millau, Henry Lemaire, Le Marché, Michelin, etc. Pierre Wynants is also the author of L'Equilibre gourmand (Les Presses de la Renaissance) and Comme chez soi (Robert Laffont), with original recipes.

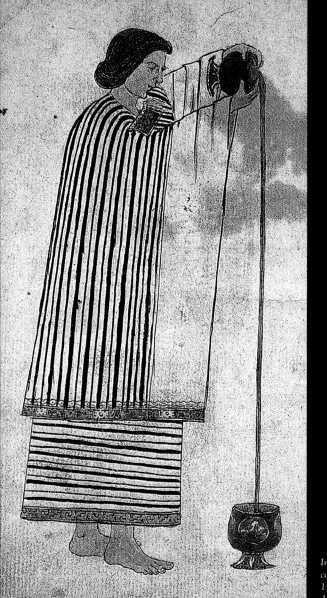

*Indian woman preparing cacao, Codex Tuleda, 1553. (Madrid, Museo de America.)*

# I. The great adventure of chocolate

*Where does chocolate come from?*
*Who was the first to grow cacao beans?*
*And what was the drink of the gods made*
*from the fruit of the cacao tree?*

*Chocolate reached Europe in the wake of*
*Christopher Columbus and gradually developed*
*into the culinary and pleasure product*
*that we know today.*

# The Discovery of Chocolate

Before the Spanish discovered America, and like other "exotic" edible products, chocolate was completely unknown in Europe. Made from the beans of the cacao trees, it was created in the pre-Colombian world.

## The Conquistadors

The year is 1502. Christopher Columbus is coming to the end of his fourth and final expedition : Cadiz, Martinique and then Guanaja, near the border with modern Honduras. The island chief, his head decorated with multicoloured feathers (the feather headdress, part of the royal regalia, was poetically known as the "shadow of lords and kings") offered him cacao beans. The native people were rightly impressed with this gift, for it was their form of currency. Among the Aztecs, a pumpkin was worth 4 cacao beans and a slave changed hands for 100 beans. Their calculations were based on a 20-base, or vigesimal, system. Four hundred beans equals 1 zontl, 20 zontls equal 1 xiquipil, and so on. Christopher Columbus took no interest in these "almonds". It was only seventeen years later, but on the Mexican coast this time, that Europeans first truly encountered chocolate.

We have reached 1519. Fernando Cortez disembarks at the head of 700 men, accompanied by horses and 14 cannon. Immediately, in his first report sent back to the Emperor Charles V, he mentions cacao : The natives consider cacao beans of such great value that they are treated like money throughout their land, to buy essentials in the markets. To the Emperor Montezuma's astonishment, Cortez would have preferred offers of gold rather than cacao beans! Cacao had always been important to the Mayans, not only for its trading value but also for its religious significance. It was stored in jars, and formed part of the funeral offerings for important dignitaries. In addition, cacao growers offered special honour to a black-faced long-

*16th century Indian offering of cacao and fruit. (The Hulton Deutsch Collection.)*

nosed god, Ek Chuah. Montezuma greeted Cortez as a god : was it not written that the snake-bird god Quetzalcoatl would return one day? According to legend he was hunted down out of jealousy by the great magician-priest Tezcatlipoca, and fled on a raft along the Tabasco coast towards the rising sun, at exactly the spot from where the Spanish caravels had appeared. But Cortez quickly realised the full "commercial" aspect of a cacao tree plantation - it could be used to obtain gold!

### The drink of the gods

The Mexicas (now known as the Aztecs) invaded the modern valley of Mexico in around AD 1300, created a new empire which stretched to the Mayan frontier, and legitimised their descent by adopting the myth of the god Quetzalcoatl. The value that they placed on cacao was symbolic as well as commercial. In Maya the word was "cacau", in the Aztec language Nahuatl it was called "cacauatl", and the drink made from it, "chaau haa", or ground cacao, became "chocoatl".

## Major dates in modern chocolate

1728 : Fry, in Bristol, is the first chocolate producer with hydraulic machinery.
1780 : Chocolate is made mecanically at Bayonne, in France.
1796 : Majani, in Bologna, is the earliest chocolate shop.
1819 : Cailler, (Swiss) makes the first chocolate bar.
1828 : Van Houten invents powdered chocolate.
1830 : Kohler develops chocolate with hazelnuts in it.
1831 : Cadbury (British) makes his own chocolate.

1901 : Suchard launches "Milka" milk chocolate.
1908 : Tobler (Swiss) creates "Toblerone".
1911 : Frank Mars gives his name to his chocolate bar.
1912 : In Belgium, Neuhaus develops the first filled chocolate, the "praline".
1913 : Séchaud markets chocolate with filling.
1915 : Jean Neuhaus patents his "ballotin" (carton) of pralines.
1921 : Kwatta launches 30 g and 45 g bars.

*Publicity poster for Manoeuvre Kwatta chocolate, 1920s.*
*(Eupen, Chocolaterie Jacques museum.)*

1832 : Franz Sacher (Austrian) invents his chocolate tart.
1846 : Fry and son launch the first tablet of dessert chocolate.
1870 : Fry launches the first chocolate bar.
1875 : Peter, with Nestlé's help, invents milk chocolate.
1879 : Lindt develops the conching process, and fondant chocolate.

1922 : G. Buitoni invents "Baci" for the Perugina company.
1923 : invention of the "Milky Way" bar.
1925 : Callebaut markets liquid *couverture* (coating) chocolate.
1930 : In the Netherlands, Nuts launches a bar with nuts and malt.
1932 : Mars reaches Europe.
1936 : Jacques markets the "baton".

What was this drink like, made from cacao beans? Around 1530 the chronicles of Gonzalo Fernandez de Oviedo give instructions on how to make it, in his *Historia general y natural de las Indias*.

Thirty beans require a pint of water. They should be roasted and finely ground. An orange-red colouring called "rocou" is added to colour the mixture and possibly to make it look like human blood. It can be drunk cold, warm or hot. Spices are usually added : vanilla, or bombax seeds.

Only the privileged few were able to enjoy this cacao drink. Montezuma himself was very fond of it. He thought it very beneficial - as an aphrodisiac, for example - and he drank it it "to go to the women". Cacao was not popular with the Spanish conquerors until the day when, short of wine, they drank it in order to avoid drinking plain water. The Milanese soldier Girolamo Benzona recorded his opinion that : "Chocoatl is fit to be thrown to the pigs".

The Emperor Montezuma in America, *Johan Ogilby, 17th century.*

### Sugar cane

The city of Tenochtilan, where Montezuma lived, was large, handsome, and well laid out. It was dominated by a large temple, the teocalli, a 114-degree pyramid. All would be destroyed by the Spanish in 1521, two years after their arrival, and the country would then be repopulated by Europeans anxious to make their fortune. This was the beginning of the colony of Mexico. And, of course, cacao trees were planted. Finally, before chocolate could become a popular drink among the colonists, it needed another ingredient in its preparation : sugar. The Spanish planted sugarcane in the Canaries, San Domingo and Mexico. Through experiments in their kitchens, monks in Oaxaca discovered the recipe for this delicious drink : it simply needed sugar, perhaps with aniseed or cinnamon. It is generally thought that the Franciscan Juan de Zumárrago, Bishop of Mexico, was the first to have mixed sugar and cocoa.

Whatever the true facts, everything immediately began to happen : "chocolaterias" opened and customers listened to music in the cool shade while enjoying frothy chocolate. Pleasures were combined.

From Mexico, chocolate spread across Spanish America : in Cuba it was "chocolate de regalo" ("festive chocolate"), with ground maize, while in Venezuela there was "chorote chocolate", with brown sugar.

# Chocolate Conquers Europe

It is a simple story: Spanish colonists returning to their own country could not bear to be without their chocolate. Not only did they bring it back with them, they brought it in shiploads to sell. This was the origin of the "Chocolate Route".

### The benefits of chocolate

Chocolate is thought to have reached Spain in 1527. Some twenty years later, Spanish merchant ships regularly took the Chocolate Route. At first, chocolate was consumed as a tonic, to improve phsyical health. Its exotic origins were intriguing and disturbing: surely it must be a magic potion? Bernard Diaz del Castillo, one of Cortez' companions, commented that "after drinking it, one can travel all day without tiring, and without needing food". The truth is that chocolate is an excellent restorative. When sugar was added to chocolate during the 1590s, the whole of Spain fell in love with it. Noble ladies drank it, even in church; they said that it enabled them to sit through long services while sustaining their weakened stomachs. This was not the opinion of the officiating priests, who were distracted by the ceaseless intrusion of servant girls bringing cups of chocolate. In the end, the ladies went to pray and drink elsewhere. Staying with the religious world, a basic question was put to Pope Clement VII: "Is chocolate a drink or a food?" In other words, did it or did it not break the fast? The answer is obvious, but it was not until 1662 that Cardinal Francesco Maria Brancaccio confirmed: "As a solid, yes; as a liquid, no".

### Antonio Carletti, the Italian

For a long time, Spanish clerical and aristocratic circles kept the delightful custom of drinking chocolate to themselves, telling no one the secret of how to make it; and they managed to hold the monopoly on it until the 17th century.

It was through his travel journal that the Italian Antonio Carletti passed on the instructions for making chocolate to his compatriots. Did he learn it directly in the West Indies, where he spent some time, or in Spain where he appreciated it in 1606? Whatever the truth may be, it was a triumph: "ciocolatieri" opened establishments almost everywhere. Skilful craftsmen, they offered chocolate in dozens of different forms, including chilled with ice or snow.

*Figure of a Moorish boy carrying a tray with a cup of chocolate. Meissen, c. 1735-40. (Liège, Musée d'Archéologie et des Arts décoratifs.)*

The city of Perugia (which was to inspire the famous "Perugina" brand) is accepted without question as the first home of the Italian taste for chocolate. Venice, however, claims to have had the first chocolate shops. It was from Italy that chocolate reached Germany ...

Nobles drinking hot chocolate in a Venetian establishment, *Giovanni Grevenbroch, late 18th century. (Venice, Museo Correr.)*

## In Germany: evening chocolate

History repeated itself, particularly in Belgium and Switzerland: a Nuremberg scientist, Johan Georg Volckammer, drank chocolate in Naples while travelling in 1641. He thoroughly enjoyed it and resolved to take some back to his own country. Even though the first Germans to taste it seem to have been somewhat cautious about a drink so different from their traditional beers, it was welcomed with tremendous enthusiasm - encouraged by its reputation as an aphrodisiac. The middle classes adopted the habit of taking a cup of chocolate before going to bed: but this reputation enjoyed by chocolate dates from the Aztec drink which was substantially peppered and spiced ...

Its reputation in this respect did not suffer. As the theologian Franciscus Rauch wrote in 1624, in Disputatio, the concoction drunk in monasteries and convents inflamed the residents" passions ...

## The English consider it extravagant ....

When chocolate reached the British Isles in 1657, it was considered an extravagance. The columns of the newspaper The Public Advertiser announced that a delicious drink could be enjoyed in Bishopsgate, in London, which came from the West Indies. For several years chocolate consumption was limited to certain restricted circles; then it spread rapidly. In 1674 it was served in the "Coffee Mill and Tobacco Roll" in London, in the form of a cake. Henry Sloane wrote a monograph on the cacao tree in 1725. Soon afterwards, King George I introduced a tax on the sale and consumption of chocolate. In 1728 Walter Churchman, in Bristol, established the first chocolate factory with hydraulic machinery. The first enthusiasts' club was founded in England in 1746! This was "The Cocoa Tree", where members tried out chocolate; they used milk instead of water, and added eggs and even wine or spirits. (It should be noted that the English language was the only one to change the basic word from the Spanish "cacao" into "cocoa"; although both versions still appear, referring to both trees and

*Poster for Rowntrees Chocolate "Elect Cocoa".*
*(Eupen, Chocolaterie Jacques museum.)*

beans, "cocoa" is used more widely, particularly for commercial and culinary reference.)

### A Royal Wedding Gift in France

Bayonne is the cradle of chocolate in France. It was here that it was introduced during the 17th century by Jews expelled from Spain. The fashion dates from October 1615 and the marriage of Louis XIII and Anne of Austria, the little Spanish Infanta. A pretty woman was observed in her retinue who was known as "Molina" because of her post at the whisk used in this remarkable

frothy drink, chocolate! (The "Molinillo" is the ridged wooden stick spun in Mexican hot chocolate to beat it to a froth.) In 1659, David Chaillou was the leading French chocolate maker. The following year, Louis XIV married Maria Theresa of Austria, the Spanish Infanta. It was said that "The king and chocolate are Maria Theresa's only passions". A royal edict in 1705 authorised lemonade sellers to sell chocolate too, and a title was even created, "Chocolate maker to the Queen", not so far removed from the title of "Supplier to the Royal Court" which is so highly prized in modern Belgium. In 1732 Dubuisson invented a flat table heated with charcoal for working chocolate. In 1778 Doret made the first hydraulic machine to pulverize cocoa beans.

### In the Grand-Place, Brussels

By then the Grand-Place in Brussels ("the finest theatre stage in the world" according to Jean Cocteau, following the same comment by Charles Baudelaire and Victor Hugo) was already the favoured place for tourists or visiting personalities. In 1697, for example, Henri Escher - mayor of Zurich - was full of

enthusiasm over the cup of chocolate that was served to him here. He imported chocolate into Switzerland, which in due course became one of the great chocolate nations through inventions such as milk chocolate and filled chocolate.

## The land of chocolate

After the death of Charles The Bold, the Low Countries were separated from Burgundy and passed through inheritance to the royal house of Spain. The conquest of the New World thus had particular repercussions in the provinces which are now Belgium. The Emperor Charles V abdicated in 1555 in favour of his son Philip II. Later, the country would be part of France, Austria and the Netherlands until 1831, when Belgium won its independence. It therefore seems entirely reasonable that the first record of a purchase of chocolate should be in the form of a gift, in the records of the Abbey of Baudeloo, in Ghent, in 1635. From its earliest history in Belgium, chocolate thus acquired the aura of a gift, to offer or to receive. It was, more precisely, the Belgian invention of praline which proved the best solution to this requirement.

## The great craftsmen of modern chocolate

• **18th century**
1770 : Paris, foundation of the "Compagnie française des chocolats et thés Pelletier et Cie".
1792 : Josty starts a chocolate company in Berne.

• **19th century**
1819 : François-Louis Caillier opens the first Swiss factory in Corsier, near Vevey.
1824 : John Cadbury opens his shop in Birmingham.
1825 : Jean-Antoine Brutus Meunier settles in Noisiel, on the River Marne.

*The Senez-Strubelle works in 1897. (Brussels, Archives de la Ville.)*

1826 : Philippe Suchard opens a chocolate factory in Neuchâtel and then at Serrières, in Switzerland.
1830 : The Swiss Charles-Amédée Kohler opens a chocolate factory.
1845 : The Meurisse chocolate factory opens in Antwerp.
1848 : Foundation of the August Poulain chocolate factory in Blois.
1848 : Foundation in Tournai of the Delannoy chocolate factory.
1849 : Inauguration of the Joveneaux chocolate factory in Tournai.
1857 : Jean Neuhaus (Swiss) settles in Brussels.

1860 : The Senez-Strubelle chocolate factory opens in Brussels.
1862 : The Quaker Henry Isaac Rowntree buys a chocolate factory in the United States.
1868 : Jean Tobler opens a chocolate factory in Berne.
1870 : Charles Neuhaus sets up a chocolate factory in Brussels, which later, under Léopold Bieswal, becomes the Côte d'Or company.
1870 : The Meyers-Courtois chocolate factory opens in Laeken.
1872 : Opening of the Delocre factory in Vilvoorde.
1879 : Rodolphe Lindt starts his business in Berne c. 1880 : Opening of Kwatta at Bois-D'Haine and Martougin in Antwerp.
1883 : Official creation of the "Côte d'Or" brand.
1884 : Alexis Séchaud opens his factory at Montreux.
1888 : The Cacao Goemare company opens in Ghent.
1889 : The Antwerp company De Beukelaere adds a chocolate and cocoa powder section to its biscuit factory.
1895 : Johann Jacobs opens a shop selling tea, coffee, chocolates and biscuits at Bremen, in Germany.
1897 : Jean-Antoine Jacques Foundation sets up a chocolate factory at Verviers.

• **20th century**
1909 : The Bruyerre company is founded at Charleroi.
1910 : Henri Wittamer opens at Le Grand Sablon in Brussels.
1911 : Callebaut adds a "chocolate" department to his factory, established in 1860.
1919 : Mlle Mary Delluc opens the "Mary" chocolate business in the Rue Royale.
1920 : M. Kestekidès launches "Léonidas".
1923 : M. Libeerts creates "Italo-Suisse" in Roulers.
1946 : Foundation of the firm of "Godiva".
1976 : Jean Galler opens his chocolate factory at Vaux-sous-Chèvremont.

# From Cacao to Chocolate

The discovery of cocoa and its crushed beans was only the first stage in the adventure of chocolate. Of course it contained cocoa paste and cocoa butter, but with the addition of sugar and/or milk.

### When the pods turn brown

Maya Indians planted cacao trees in the northern part of Latin America by around 600 BC. According to legend, the first beans came from paradise and bestowed wisdom on anyone who ate them, which explains the emperors' concern to retrict their use. The trees only grow in humid, warm and shady zones, preferaby at altitudes of less than 600 m - i.e. the tropical zone lying between 22 degrees north, on a level with Cuba, and 21 degrees south, in line with the island of Réunion. Trees are prevented from growing taller than 8 m (unchecked, they can reach 14 m!), so that the pods can be picked more easily. Each pod, the fruit of the cacao tree, contains around fifty beans. The pod is a type of thick shell, 30 cm long, which changes colour as it ripens, from green and yellow to orange, red and brown. It is a valuable and highly-developed species, for out of the 6,000 flowers on a cacao tree only 1 per cent develop into a pod. They are gathered twice a year, in June and in October.

*Crushing and shelling of cocoa beans. (Vervier, Chocolaterie Jacques, early 20th century.)*

### Cacao Producers

In the 19th century, as European manufacturing expanded and flourished, cacao trees were introduced into Equador, Brazil and Africa (in 1822): the Ivory Coast, Brazil, Ghana, Nigeria and Cameroon came to be the world's leading producers, with figures varying between 100 and 530 thousand tonnes of beans annually (out of a total of 2.4 million tonnes). We know that in 1830 the world production was only 10,000 tonnes!

Today, when the cacao tree has been introduced into Asia, the three leading producers on the world market are the Ivory Coast, Brazil and Malaysia. When the sacks of beans reach the chocolate manufacturer, they are spread out for several days and turned over in the sun to develop their aroma to its maximum. They may be yellowish-brown (criollos) or brownish-purple (forasteros). Another type of bean (trinatarios), a cross between these two, grows in Trinidad.

*Cacao-tree plantation at Kiniati in 1941. (Brussels, Musée Royal de l'Afrique Centrale.)*

Dark chocolate consists of cocoa paste, cocoa butter and sugar. Milk chocolate is simply made by adding ... milk. White chocolate consists of cocoa butter, sugar and milk.

### The Alchemy of Chocolate

The quality of chocolate depends on the selection of the beans. The first secret of manufacturing is the proportion of bean varieties. Each type of cocoa has its own scent and flavour, its own subtleties. For many years, for example, the finest mixture possible seemed to be a blend of two-thirds Brazilian "maragnan" to one-third Venezuelan "caraque". A small amount of "cayenne" was included, to add a little individual savour: entirely a matter of taste, even of good taste.

Once this early decision has been made, the alchemy of all the subsequent operations is delicate and complex. The proportion of cocoa butter produces a chocolate which is more or less dry, and the proportion of sugar makes it more or less sweet. The bitter element of dark chocolate should be positive, never neutral. Yet

### Chocolate Paste

Three major operations are needed to transform the beans into a paste:

• torrefaction, or roasting: exposed to hot air, at a temperature of between 120-140 degrees, the beans separate out from their shells. The flavour intensifies;

• crushing: the beans turn into a soft paste or "mass", cocoa paste. This is a suspension of cocoa solids in cocoa butter. Sugar is added, and at this point a decision must be made, since after these processes the paste is ready to go in one of two directions, to become either cocoa powder or chocolate. Cocoa powder is made by alkalizing the paste, then pulverising and homogenising it before taking off the cocoa butter (which will be used in preparing chocolate) from the "cake", or remaining solids (which will be crushed into powder);

• conching: the paste is tipped into large vats at a temperature varying between 50 and 80 degrees. Cocoa butter is added to make it more fluid: the result is chocolate.

this brings us into the domain of the subjective, where even the vocabulary used, as for a wine, is a matter of personal judgement. A chocolate can be irritating or bitter, sharp or refreshing. It can the earthy colour of burnt amber, or darkly violet-tinted. Its aroma may be sensual or exotic. To the touch, it may be powdery, melting, firm, yielding ...

*"Tapoteuses" tapping the moulds in a chocolate factory, early 20th century.*

### How Chocolate is made

Chocolate paste is kept in its liquid state, at a temperature of 40 degrees. To make it into baton form, for example. it is chilled to 10 degrees so that the cocoa butter becomes completely crystallised. Then it is poured into a mould, preheated to 27 degrees, which will retain its brilliance. The moulds are tapped, to shake out any air bubbles. The chocolate passes through cooling tunnels so that first the outside and then the centre can harden. The mould is heated once more to blend all together, and chilled again before the finished batons are taken out of the mould.

### Chocolate in Europe

Three types of chocolate are officially recognised:
• Dark, or fondant, chocolate, also known simply as "chocolate"
• milk chocolate
• white chocolate

The minimum level of pure cocoa allowed in chocolate is 35 per cent, according to European standards (in Belgium this rises to 43 per cent).

In some countries in the European Union (Austria, Denmark, Finland, Sweden, Norway, Ireland, Great Britain and Portugal), between 3 and 15 per cent of the cocoa butter can be replaced by less costly vegetable fats. A proposed European directive aims to standardise this norm. Since July 1995 Switzerland has agreed that other vegetable fats can replace 5 per cent of cocoa butter. These fats are palm, rape (colza) or soya oil, or mahua (illipe) or karite nut butters, all less expensive than cocoa.

The new directive will have certain consequences:
• the manufacturing cost of chocolate will be lower with vegetable fats other than cocoa butter;
• cocoa-producing countries (the Ivory Coast, for example, which produces nearly one-third of the world's cocoa) may see a drop in their national income;
• if some chocolate manufacturers wish to continue using only cocoa

in large quantities, should there be a special name, a new protection in the form of a special label? (In the case of milk chocolate, for example, the law specifies that if it contains at least 30 per cent cocoa, the maker can call it "superior quality".)

### The great inventions
It was the Dutchman Conrad J. Van Houten who was responsible for one of the great inventions in the modern history of chocolate: powdered chocolate. In 1828 he invented a press which extracted the cocoa butter, where formerly a beater was needed to make the liquid frothy.

Chocolate with nuts in it was made in 1830 by the Swiss Charles-Amédée Kohler, who later joined forces with Daniel Peter. In 1875 Peter created milk chocolate, which he made by the process of condensing milk, developed by another famous Swiss citizen,

*Wrapping. (Chocolaterie Jacques, Verviers, early 20th century.)*

Henri Nestlé. The first filled chocolate was "invented" in 1912 by Jean Neuhaus. The praline, as Neuhaus named it, became the foundation of the Belgian chocolate trade. In Chicago the American chocolate maker Mars gave his name to the famous bar in 1911 at Tacoma (Washington). In 1923 he launched the "Milky Way" bar which created fashion for filled chocolate bars. In 1932 his son, Forrest Mars Jnr, perfected *the* Mars Bar as we know it today.

*Publicity poster for Van Houten cocoa.*
*(London, Mary Evans Picture Library.)*

# Chocolate in all its variety

The definition of chocolate is: "Product obtained from cocoa beans, in paste or powder form, or skimmed cocoa powder, with sugar, with or without the addition of cocoa butter, at least 14 per cent of defatted dry cocoa and 18 per cent of cocoa butter."

### Chocolate bars

Chocolate exists in four types of bar: chocolate, milk chocolate, white chocolate and filled chocolate. The chocolate coating for the latter must form at least one-quarter of the total weight. In chocolates and milk chocolates, other descriptions are used according to their proportion of cocoa, with "cooking chocolate" having a minimum of 30 per cent cocoa, "chocolate" with a minimum of 35 per cent, and "superior chocolate" with a minimum of 43 per cent cocoa.

### "Couverture" Chocolate

"Couverture" (coating) chocolate is the form used as a raw material for chocolate manufacturers, confectioners and pastry chefs. It contains at least 31 per cent of cocoa butter and 12.5 per cent of defatted dry cocoa. While couverture chocolate is traditionally kept at temperatures below 18 degrees, causing problems of storage space and cooling power, Charles Callebaut had the bright idea of keeping it in a warm and liquid state. This raw material

*Trembleuse chocolate cup, 18th century.*
*(Antwerp, Kunsthistorische musea,*
*Museum Smidt Van Gelder.)*

can be delivered in tanker-lorries fitted with heat recovery systems. Smaller chocolate manufacturers can also make use of these high quality products.

### Fillings

Fillings come in infinite variety, but there are of course some classics:

- fondant: a sugar syrup with added glucose, worked with a spatula until it is white and malleable. It is flavoured with coffee, vanilla or fruit;
- ganache: a mixture of heated fresh cream and chocolate, sometimes with added liqueur, tea or fruit;
- gianduja: a paste based on oily fruits such as almonds, hazelnuts or pistachios, finely crushed with sugar and chocolate;
- praline: a mixture of toasted almonds or hazelnuts, and caramelised sugar. In most cases these two are added in equal quantities. Fillings are also made with nougat, almond paste, fruit paste, peppermint cream, liqueurs, etc.

### Chocolate Riches

Chocolate is extremely nutritious. It is rich in sugar and fats, and also contains mineral salts - magnesium and iron. (A 10 g bar of dark chocolate eaten with 100 g of bread gives a child of between 4 and 11 about one-third of his daily requirement of magnesium). Milk chocolate naturally has more calcium, but it contains less magnesium. Finally, chocolate has tonic qualities, for it contains theobromine and a little caffeine, which stimulate the human central nervous system. The word "theobromine" (with the Greek meaning of "food of the gods") is derived from the scientific name of the cocoa tree, "Theobroma cacao L", given to it by Carl Linnaeus himself in the 18th century.

### Erotic Chocolate
In his 1702 treatise on food, Louis Lemery wrote of chocolate that "its qualities as a stimulant would excite the ardour of Venus". The Viennese doctor Johann Michael Haider always referred to it as "Veneris Pabullum", or the food of Venus.

### A Passion for Chocolate
Chocolate makers, manufacturers as well as craftsmen, are men of passion, stimulated by the extraordinary adventure of transforming a raw material into a delicious foodstuff. This trade demands unfailing professionalism, accurate and detailed knowledge and, for those who expe-

rience it as a passion, an artist's soul. For these reasons it generally attracts people with a vocation. Creative craftsmen can compare themselves with composers, artists, poets, with all those who harness a mysterious alchemy to move from a word to a line, from a series of notes to a symphony, from a cocoa bean to a praline with a unique flavour ... This technical skill, this rigour, this savoir-faire and invention are recognised and approved by the public with a passion for particu-

*Jean-Michel Moreau le Jeune, Le Lever, 18th century. (Paris, Petit Palais.)*

lar brands of chocolate and particular salons where they may be enjoyed. And since we are concerned with passion, we should also consider shared pleasure. How can the chocolate consumer explain such a passion? Is it rational? The great gastronome Brillat-Savarin said, "Fortunate chocolate which, having covered the world through women's smiles, comes to its end in a delectable melting kiss in their mouth."

In one of the short stories in his *Contes de la Bécasse*, Guy de Maupassant writes, "I have never drunk anything like it! Chocolate that you would die for, rich, velvety, scented, intoxicating. I could not take the delicious cup from my mouth". Passion is a synonym for excess. Franquin's Gaston Lagaffe added a spoonful of hot chocolate to the oil anointing his Chantilly sardines!

### Chocolate as Aphrodisiac
In the 17th century the English poet James Wadsworth wrote lines in honour of chocolate and its stimulating virtues:

*Wrapping for Théobroma chocolate, referring to a "god of chocolate".*

"It makes old women young and fresh once more,
And stirs their flesh with tremors of delight,
It brings them sighing for your secret gifts,
When once they know the precious taste of chocolate."

At the end of the same century, certain guides suggested that egg whites and other "cantharides" should be replaced with the aphrodisiac ingredient of chocolate. In the following century, chocolate appeared high on the list of dishes thought to favour amorous encounters. The list mentions game, marrow-bones, oysters, caviare - and champagne and chocolate. No doubt the luxurious and glamorous atmosphere surrounding their consumption has a share in their effect. Madame du Barry always offered a cup of whipped chocolate to her lovers. Casanova observed in his memoirs that whipped chocolate struck him as more effective in reviving his vigour than champagne!

## Chocolate ... a poison?

The famous "divine" Marquis Donatien Alphonse François de Sade regularly organised evening parties at Marseille to which he invited local beauties. He had the gruesome and perverse notion of giving these ladies pieces of chocolate which were filled with can-tharidine (extract of cantharides, an insect found widely in the south of France), a powerful congestive alcaloid ... Madame de Pompadour regularly drank cups of ambered chocolate to warm her blood: grey amber has the reputation of being an aphrodisiac. In his recipe book *Cuisine antidéprime* ("antidepressant cooking"), Sylvain Lebel writes that "chocolate is a mythic food, to be ranked alongside forbidden fruit".

## The Sensuality of Chocolate

Chocolate clearly harbours elements of eroticism and sensuality. It arouses all the senses:

• visual: it may have a matt, glossy or satiny surface; the rich range of colours runs from black to red and to brown. White chocolate should always be ivory-coloured;

• taste: the four primary savours can be identified: sweet, salty, acid and bitter. Chocolate gives off its aromas most strongly at temperatures between 18 and 21 degrees. It should be smooth, melting only in the mouth;

• touch: like a fabric, chocolate can be soft or harsh, substantial or light ...;

• hearing: it can crack, crunch, or creak. The sound of breaking chocolate should be a dry snap. If the piece crumbles, it is too old and if it breaks badly it does not have a sufficiently high proportion of cocoa butter;

• scent: of course vanilla, coffee or nougat flavours can be identified by the nose, but when it is in the mouth chocolate can yield savours which are appreciated retronasally - woody, toasted or praline notes.

There is an art in tasting chocolate, just as with wine or cookery. And the setting in which chocolate is offered is equally important. In 1901 Thomas Mann wrote in *Buddenbrooks*: "The fresh morning air drifted in through the open french windows, and instead of coffee and tea, a cup of chocolate was served".

### Wine and Chocolate

Chocolate, a rich food and complex in its variety, is not easy to combine with drinks. Water is the classic partner specified by the fathers of twentieth century gastronomy (Escoffier, Curnonsky, Dumas). Coffee is also a good

*Antonio de Pereda y Salgado*, Still Life. *(1652 Saint Petersburg, Hermitage Museum.)*

and versatile companion, particularly when vanilla is included in the composition of the chocolate. When it comes to wines, the definitive incompatible pairing is undoubtedly that of champagne and chocolate. In general, the partnership with wine depends essentially on the type of chocolate.

These are the suggestions of Eric Boschman (Le Pain et le Vin, 812 chaussée d'Alsemberg, 1180 Uccle) one of Belgium's greatest specialists:

• milk chocolate: sweet white wines, such as a Jura straw wine or a sweet sherry. Certain dry red wines: a Saint-Emilion which is not too strongly marked by tannins, or an old Rioja. To accompany a milk chocolate dessert with fruit such as apricots or peaches: a young Sauternes or a Lipari malmsey. Milk chocolate does not go well with naturally sweet red wines such as porto, Maury or Banyuls;

• dark chocolate (approximately around 60 per cent cocoa solids): the most obvious partner is a naturally sweet red wine, fairly well aged or at least slightly oxidised, such as a tawny port or ten-year-old Banyuls. For a strong effect, a relatively fruity cognac or a slightly smoky single malt whisky is the answer. Certain white wines made in the same way, such as Tokay, Passito de Panteleria, sweet marsala or golden Rivesaltes also make a sound partnership.

If dark chocolate is used in preparing a dessert or pâtisserie, its accompaniment must first be considered. For a purée of red fruit, look for a relatively light red wine, perhaps slightly sparkling, such as a Brachetto from Piedmont or a Cerdon from Bugey. For crème anglaise (an egg custard), a better selection would be a white wine, slightly oxidised and sweet or, for a bold choice, a yellow wine from the Jura. When it is a matter of a chocolate dessert with mint-flavoured egg custard, the only solution is a herbal tisane ...

• bitter dark chocolate: the king of chocolates is the easiest to match. At room temperature it goes perfectly with unoxidised sweet red wines such as vintage port, vintage Maury, Rimatge Banyuls or even Virgen Malaga wine. For those who prefer spirits, a reasonably well-aged cognac with spicy aromas, a well aged single malt whisky or a fine Calvados will gently complement its savour. No white wines, except in the case of certain types of pâtisserie.

Gérard Boyer, of the Château des Crayères at Reims, creates a bitter chocolate tart which goes perfectly with vintage Krug champagne; but this, in my opinion, is the exception which proves the rule.

*Liqueur assortment by Neuhaus*

I. The great adventure of chocolate

As with all pleasures, chocolate carries an image of guilt. It's so good, it must be a sin, as people often say ! Is it bad? I don't know ... Is it bad for the health? That's another question. Look at it methodically and above all, remember that it should be eaten in moderation. We look at these problems in the company of Dr Karin Rondia ("Pulsations" on RTBF).

• Chocolate is high in calories
As can be seen in the chart of its nutritional value, it is a high-energy food. Will Tura is right to eat it before he goes jogging. As commented above, it is important to be reasonable, particularly those who tend towards plumpness. Cocoa powder contains 312 calories per 100 g, dark chocolate 512 and milk chocolate 528.

• Chocolate does not affect the liver
In fact, contrary to widely-accepted opinion, it is not the liver which is affected by over-indulgence, but the biliary tract, for the good reason that the bile duct is the organ designed to ease digestion of high-fat foods. If it increases in size it becomes painful.

• Chocolate has no effect on
the cholesterol level
As it contains a proportion of fatty acids, it has been thought that it encourages cholesterol : this is wrong. Dark chocolate has no effect; milk chocolate has between 15 and 18 mg per 100 g. In other words, it has no effect.

• Chocolate does not cause acne
No study has ever been able to link chocolate and acne. Similarly, with the over-fatty food often eaten by children (chips, hamburgers, etc.), there is no proof that this type of diet is linked with acne.

• Chocolate does not cause allergies
This only happens exceptionally rarely.

• Chocolate does not cause migraine
Only for those predisposed to migraines, who may find them intensified by chocolate.

• Chocolate does not encourage constipation
It is wrong to say that chocolate encourages constipation. It contains no fibre and is therefore not laxative either.

*Book by one of Louis XIV's doctors.*

• Chocolate causes tooth decay
This may be true of poor quality chocolate which contains too much sugar !

• Chocolate is not aphrodisiac
It is known that the Aztecs drank a chocolate which was aphrodisiac, because it was blended with pimento. Sugar has replaced the savoury pimento. Chocolate contains a substance which helps to rouse the emotions, but in such tiny quantities that the consequences can never be sexual.

• Chocolate is not a drug
Those who say they cannot do without it are concerned with psychological dependence. Similarly, people may be "hooked" by television or crossword puzzles ! Thus, people eat chocolate when they are anxious or feel unloved. This is because chocolate is a pleasure - always an important feature - and brings a feeling of calm, serenity, a pause in the hurly-burly of life. As for the famous theobromine and caffeine in chocolate, they may no doubt give an added something to the body, if needed.

We should be aware, therefore, that virtually none of the negative points survive the analysis; on the contrary, chocolate's richness in minerals - magnesium, potassium, iron - should be emphasised. Enough, surely, to silence its detractors and reassure the anxious, or dieting enthusiasts.

Jean-Anthelme Brillat-Savarin (1755-1826) was the author of *La Physiologie du goût* (The Physiology of Taste). His name has been bestowed on a cheese, but it could have been given to a chocolate ! He wrote : "People who eat chocolate are those who enjoy a more ordinarily sound state of health and are the least liable to suffer a mass of minor ills which detract from the enjoyment of life."

And Doctor Karin Rondia declares : "I adore chocolate. But I am reasonable about it; I never eat a whole bar at once, and I choose good quality pralines. At home, I always have a supply of good chocolate in the cupboard, which I eat with tea or coffee. Like everyone else, it's when I'm feeling "down" or when I'm particularly hungry that I eat it ..."

## How to look after chocolate

**• Temperature**
It should be constant, between 4 and 8 degrees. If it is taken from heat to cold, chocolate becomes paler. Going from cold to warm, it sweats. And if the temperature is too high, it turns lighter in colour - and then it melts.

**• Humidity**
This bleaches the chocolate. A damp storage place is not suitable.

**• Smell**
Chocolate is best kept in a closed container or aluminium foil, to prevent it absorbing other strong scents.

*Vanilla pods*

*Cacao plant with its pod open*

*Cinnamon sticks*

## The nutritional value of chocolate

Average composition of 100 g of chocolate

| Ingredients | Dark chocolate | Milk chocolate |
|---|---|---|
| **• Nutritional ingredients** | | |
| Proteins | 3,2 g | 7,6 g |
| Lipids | 33,5 g | 32,3 g |
| Carbohydrate | 60,3 g | 53,0 g |
| Pure Lecithin | 0,3 g | 0,3 g |
| Alkaloids (theobromine) | 0,6 g | 0,2 g |
| **• Minerals** | | |
| Calcium | 20 mg | 220 mg |
| Magnesium | 80 mg | 50 mg |
| Phosphate | 130 mg | 210 mg |
| **• Trace Elements** | | |
| Iron | 2,0 mg | 0,8 mg |
| Copper | 0,7 mg | 0,4 mg |

| Ingredients | Dark chocolate | Milk chocolate |
|---|---|---|
| **• Vitamins** | | |
| A | 40 U.I. | 300 U.I. |
| B1 | 0,06 mg | 0,1 mg |
| B2 | 0,06 mg | 0,3 mg |
| C | 1,14 mg | 70 U.I. |
| D | 50 U.I. | 70 U.I. |
| E | 2,4 mg | 1,2 mg |
| **• Available energy** | | |
| Calories | 495 | 515 |

(Source : Institut de recherches du café et du cacao-IRCC)

I. The great adventure of chocolate

*"The finest of fine chocolate"* (Poulain).

# "PLEASURE BY THE SQUARE" (NESTLÉ).

*"A chocolate of infinite tenderness"* (Lindt).

*"Tenderly chocolate"* (Milka).

# *"Passionately"* (Lanvin).

**"From rich smooth chocolate, Suchard knows how to draw out every pleasure"** (Suchard).

*"The real thing is best !"* (Callebaut).

# **"A taste of paradise" (Bounty).**

# "FOR A ROAR OF PLEASURE" (LION).

"You will let yourself be tempted ..." (Mars).

## *"Plan your night-time with the taste of the dark" (Nestlé).*

## "You have never known such feelings" (Lindt).

*IN BELGIUM, "PRALINE" MEANS "FINE FILLED CHOCOLATE" AND "NEUHAUS" MEANS "THE FINEST PRALINES" (NEUHAUS).*

*Building the Matadi-Stanley Pool railway, a significant stage in the history of Belgian chocolate, in 1892-1898*

# II. The Great Adventure of Praline

After it reached Europe, chocolate came
to be eaten in the distinctive form of pralines,
a name derived from the Marshal du
Plessis-Praslin.

It was the great Belgian promoters such
as Jean Neuhaus who developed the product
until it became the pralines that we
know today.

We must understand what we mean by "a praline". The French dictionary gives it two definitions: either a toasted almond or hazelnut covered with sugar icing (known in Belgium as "christening sugar") or, in Belgium, an individual chocolate, usually filled. While noting that in Switzerland the same confection is known as a "bouchée au chocolat" ("chocolate mouthful"), it is the Belgian meaning that is used here. There is no legal definition of praline, because of the great range of applications.

### The Duc du Plessis-Praslin

The first spelling of the word, in 1662, was "prasline". It was written "praline" in 1680. The name comes from the Maréchal du Plessis-Praslin, whose chef Lassagne invented almonds tossed in a small amount of boiling sugar. Monsieur de Choiseul, Duc du Plessis-Praslin (1598-1675) was an ambassador from the court of the French King Louis XIII. Sent to suppress the people of Bordeaux who were in rebellion against the king's authority, he asked Lassagne to invent a delicacy which

would distract the rebels. Seeing one of his kitchen boys scrape up and nibble a little piece of melted sugar, he had the idea of "prasline". Having won his claim to glory, the marshal retired to Montargis where he founded the "Maison de la praline", the House of Praline, which still exists today.

Box of pralines, c. 1880.

### Jean Neuhaus Invents Modern Praline

Founded in 1857, the pharmaceutical confectionery Neuhaus business already used chocolate for many of its creations. On the death of Frédéric Neuhaus in 1895, his son Jean (bearing the same fore-name as his grandfather, who came from Neuchâtel in Switzerland) took over the confectioner's shop in the Galerie de la Reine in Brussels. Although he intended to be an engineer, Frédéric brought a new energy to the family business. Louise Agostini, his wife, helped him. From her sculptor great-grandfather she inherited a definite artistic talent; she it was who undertook changes in the shop, looked after the decoration, and designed the Napoleonic "N" which became the firm's acknowledged emblem. She helped her husband to create the famous praline. We have reached 1912; praline is a filling surrounded by chocolate. (On this point, it may be imagined that the word "praline" attracted Neuhaus also for its agricultural meaning: a mixture in which seeds are soaked and coated before sowing.) In 1915 Jean Neuhaus took out a patent in Brussels, with the sample of an industrial model wrapped in a chocolate box. This was the famous "ballotin" or carton for pralines, which came to be a useful replacement for cornet packets which crushed the sweets inside them.

### Making Praline

Although praline making is partly mechanised, part of the work, and particularly the decoration, is still done by hand. Two techniques are used, depending on the type of filling.

*Moulage*, or moulding: liquid chocolate is poured into a hollow mould, and the containers chilled to set the chocolate. They are filled with liquid or thick filling, and sealed with a layer of liquid chocolate which forms the underside of the praline. They are unmoulded after further chilling.
*Enrobage*, or coating: the filling is dipped in a bath of liquid chocolate, or passed through a curtain of chocolate. This allows for a very wide range of praline flavours, depending partly on the type of chocolate – milk, white, etc. – and partly on the filling - cream, marzipan, etc.

*Making fine pralines. (Chocolaterie Jacques, Verviers, early 20th century.)*

## The Classic Pralines

Belgium has a distinctive and very successful tradition of pralines sold individually so that customers can make their own selection. They are sold in specialised shops and by certain confectionery and pâtisserie shops. Four classic varieties are most often found on sale:

• Praline milk chocolate: the filling consists of sugar, almonds and/or hazelnuts, sometimes even toasted cashew nuts, a small amount of vanilla, cocoa and/or cocoa butter, all coated in milk chocolate.
• Fondant chocolate and fresh cream or butter: the fondant chocolate surrounds a filling of fresh cream or butter cream.
• Manon: a large praline filled with fresh cream or butter and a walnut kernel. The coating consists of white chocolate or fondant sugar, sometimes coffee-flavoured. This praline is a major topic of discussion; for some people it should be covered with fondant sugar, for others it should be white chocolate. The important point is not to compare them:

they are two different pralines. But if they are made with fondant sugar, they should not be over-sweetened. The covering layer (which should be glossy, not brittle) should not be too thick. If they are coated with white chocolate, they will be smaller. Some praline manufacturers do not use white chocolate, under the pretence that it is not a complete chocolate: the true reason for this, however, is the greater difficulty of finding flavours which blend well with this type of chocolate without creating a sickly result.

• fondant chocolate and marzipan: fondant chocolate surrounds a filling of marzipan, sometimes with the addition of nuts or preserved fruit, or flavoured with pistachio.

It should be recognised that the more complex the decoration of a praline, the more labour it requires and therefore the higher the cost.

### The Ideal Range of Pralines

Good praline makers should offer an ideal range of pralines. Too

Diderot, Encyclopaedia, *the confectioner's equipment. (Eupen, Chocolaterie Jacques museum).*

often they only have a very large range of one type and neglect all others. A good sample should include at least one praline in each of the eight major categories listed below, and each of them in each colour (fondant, milk and white), totalling 24 types.

• Marzipan: this is a blend of almonds and sugar. Good marzipan is made with freshly blanched almonds. Although the almond content is often 30 per cent, the right proportion is 50 or 60 per cent.

• Praline: this is a mixture of toasted hazelnuts or almonds, and caramelised sugar.

• Gianduja: a mixture of toasted nuts and white sugar. Gianduja is half-way between marzipan and praline: it has white sugar, as in marzipan, and toasted nuts as in praline, but with the addition of either cocoa butter or chocolate.

• Truffle: a mixture of butter, fondant sugar, chocolate, and often a liqueur. The butter is often replaced by margarine, or there may be too much sugar. What is required is that when the truffle is placed on the tongue, it melts on its own …

• Fresh cream: as the name indicates, the main ingredient is fresh cream; but it also has fondant sugar, a little butter and a little alcohol, for freshness and to help it keep fresh longer.

• Ganache: this is a mixture of heated fresh cream and chocolate, with sometimes the addition of a liqueur, tea or fruit.

• Fondant: as such, it is little used in good-quality pralines. It is part of the manufacture of other kinds of sweets, such as cherries in kirsch, truffles, or pralines with fresh cream.

• Liqueur: some pralines, made with fresh cream, ganache, praline, truffle or marzipan, include a liqueur. The true liqueur praline comes in two types: with a crust which, when bitten into, releases three flavours - the liqueur, the chocolate and, between the two, a fine flake of crystallised sugar; and without a crust, with similar ingredients but without the crystallised sugar.

*Basin designed to keep chocolate hot, 1890.*

In the particular case of cherries in Kirsch, the cherry (without its stone) must be set in a translucent syrup. The barely sweetened chocolate balances the sweetness of the syrup. The danger in this praline (and for liqueurs in general) is that the fine underlying layer of chocolate is lost.

### How to choose a praline

The choice of a praline is of course a matter of personal taste. It is possible, however, to suggest a certain number of objective criteria to help the customer in search of quality.

### The Praline Shop

Because this is a food, the shop must be clean. The chocolates must be displayed in a clear light. The temperature surrounding the chocolates must be

*Liqueur pralines being packed by hand. (Vanparys workshops, Brussels, 1922.)*

constant, to keep them in good condition. The sales staff, who must always use gloves when handling the pralines, should have a good knowledge and understanding of their range of products, in order to guide the customer.

### Presentation of the Pralines
The carton should be included in the sale price - even when the container is of high quality and

special shape. The pralines should always be carefully placed inside the package, so that they can be sent or carried without risk: for example, layers of pralines should be carefully separated. The following information should be provided on the outside of the carton, or inside it:
• the manufacturer's address
• advice on keeping the contents fresh
• the final date for eating them

*Orange and dark chocolate.*

### The Quality of the Pralines
The first question is, why do some praline makers not sell white chocolate pralines ? The pretext that it is not a matter of chocolate is not the true reason. It is often a matter of skill. Indeed, it is more of a challenge to find flavours which go well with white chocolate without creating an excessively sweet product. But it is also true that any lack of hygiene shows up more quickly with white chocolate!

There are a few ways in which a praline can be tested quickly:

• colour: white chocolate should show a tendency towards off-white and buff tones. Milk chocolate should be neither too light nor too dark. Its colouring should be smooth and unbroken. Finally, dark chocolate should be deep and intense in colour;

• Shine: a praline should be glossy, with gleaming mirror effects for a moulded praline and a satiny sheen for a coated praline.

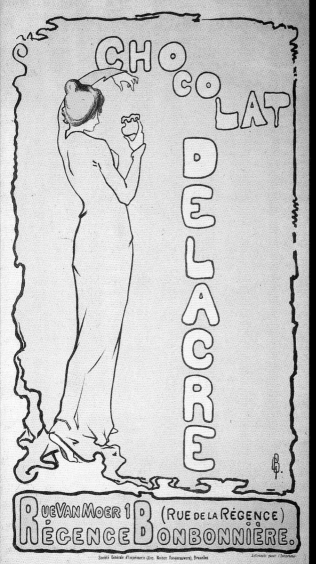

CHOCOLAT DELACRE

Société Générale d'Imprimerie (Anc. Maison Vanderauwera), Bruxelles

Affichette pour l'Intérieur

Rue Van Moer 1 B (Rue de la Régence)
Régence Bonbonnière.

*Publicity poster for Delacre chocolate. (Eupen, Chocolaterie Jacques museum.)*

• the shell: it should be the finest and most regular possible. A chocolate which is well balanced in its raw materials and well worked will break cleanly;

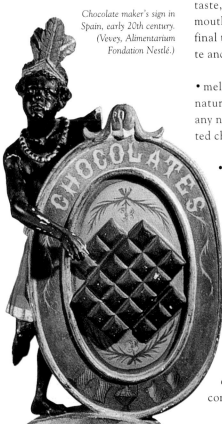

*Chocolate maker's sign in Spain, early 20th century. (Vevey, Alimentarium Fondation Nestlé.)*

• flavour: a praline should have a natural aroma and no scent of artificial extract, which is generally sickly and too pronounced. The taste moves rapidly through three stages: the first flavour, the main taste, and the after-taste in the mouth and on the palate - but the final taste should still be chocolate and not sugar;

• melting: pralines should have a natural tendency to melt without any need for salivation and repeated chewing;

• decoration: it should be edible without affecting the praline taste.

If all these characteristics are achieved you will feel encouraged to eat the whole carton at one sitting, to tell your friends where to find good pralines, and to return to the shop - not only to buy more of what you have already enjoyed, but to embark with confidence on new flavours!

*Chocolate maker's sign in Milan, c. 1859. (Milan museum.)*

# III. Belgian chocolate makers

Chocolate's favourite country, Belgium has had a large number of chocolate industrialists in its recent history, who have developed product lines, brands and dynamic economic activity.

The enterprising spirit of these nineteenth-century pioneers has turned chocolate into a national emblem and one of Belgian gastronomy's most famous products.

For many reasons, Belgium is "the land of chocolate". For the quality of its products, undoubtedly: the smoothness of texture, the quality/price relationship, the raw materials used. And for skill and the enthusiasm of craft workers, both large and small scale, even more undisputably ! Amy, a character in David Lodge's bestseller Therapy, describes to her psychiatrist a recent episode with her lover, who asks: "'Was it all right for you?" Of course I said it was wonderful, though to be honest, I've had more pleasure from a nice hot bath at the end of a long day, or a really top-class Belgian chocolate with a cup of freshly-ground Colombian coffee. Frankly.'

## When chocolate goes well ...

The Belgian chocolate industry is in increasingly good health. It has been advancing steadily for the last ten years. Overall, it has risen from 146,000 tonnes in 1984 to 340,000 tonnes in 1993. The most spectacular rise is in couverture, or coating chocolate, which accounts for 10 per cent of the increase. Two-thirds of couverture chocolate is destined for the export market, with France, the Netherlands and Germany the principal purchasers. (Belgium sold chocolate to the French to the value of 6.5 million Belgian francs in 1957; in 1992 the figure was 6.6 billion Belgian francs... ) In the finished chocolate sector, white chocolate has dropped while dark chocolate has leaped forward by 70 per cent. The three most substantial clients outside Europe are, in order of commercial significance, the United States, Canada and Australia.

## Belgian Production

Chocolate manufacturing employs 7,000 workers in Belgium, in 94 establishments with more than 5 workers. Each Belgian province except Namur has at least one production centre in its territory. The province of Antwerp has the most: 32.

The Flemish region lists 73 businesses, there are 13 in the Walloon region and 8 in the Brussels region. When it comes to turnover, two giants stand out at the head of chocolate-making establishments: Callebaut, with a turnover of 19.2 billion Belgian francs in 1995, and Kraft-Jacobs

*Advertising poster for Menier chocolate, 1892. (Brussels, Archives de la Ville.)*

### Development of consumption

The pattern of consumption per household of chocolate, ice cream and confectionery shows an impressive rise over the last 20 years. The INS offers three points of comparison: the years 1977-78, 1987-88 and 1995-96:

1977 . . . . . . . . . . 4,221 BF
1987 . . . . . . . . . . 5,878 BF
1996 . . . . . . . . . . 7,661 BF

This represents the average expenditure per household, per year. Although this is far from the record of expenditure of food products, held by meat (for which the 1996 figure is 21,196 BF), chocolate none the less ranks equal with the amount spent on milk (7,225 BF in 1996). This average of chocolate consumption can be further analysed at 7,908 BF for the Flemish region, 7,804 BF for the Walloon region and only 5,958 BF for the Brussels region.

with a turnover of 12.8 billion Belgian francs. We should, finally, note that Belgium is the world's leading cocoa importer, importing 6 per cent of total cocoa volume (a total of 2.5 million tonnes, with 60 per cent produced in Africa) to a population which represents 0.2 per cent of world population ! Europe consumes 60 per cent of the world cocoa production.

## Belgians as leaders

Regions of Italy and the future Belgium were the first to develop a taste for chocolate, well ahead of the French, who did not follow the example of their queens Anne of Austria and Marie-Thérèse. Amsterdam was the natural delivery port for the cacao. In the 17th century it was the Dutch who overtook the Spanish in running the best commercial sea transport system.

In 1735 the house journal *Amusemens* (sic) of the Spa waters recounted that diners had added a little opium to the chocolate served after dinner, in order to dispose of a boring fellow diner. It was their way of neutralising the killjoy when the dancing began ...

### Modern chocolate production - the important figures

| | | |
|---|---|---|
| Snacks (confectionery bars) | 24 600 t | (30 %) |
| Pralines | 18 000 t | (22 %) |
| Bars | 12 100 t | (15 %) |
| Batons | 9 700 t | (12 %) |
| Seasonal items | 4 700 t | |
| Small pieces | 2 200 t | |
| Other items | 2 100 t | |
| Couverture chocolate (production) | 180 000 t | |

*Côte d'Or beach bucket wrappers for chocolate bouchées.*

### Chocolate consumption in Europe

Per head per year

| | | | |
|---|---|---|---|
| 1. Switzerland | 8,8 kg | 6. The Netherlands | 6,8 kg |
| 2. Great Britain | 8,0 kg | 7. Austria | 6,7 kg |
| 3. Norway | 7,8 kg | 8. Ireland | 5,7 kg |
| 4. Germany | 6,8 kg | 9. Denmark | 5,7 kg |
| 5. Belgium | 6,8 kg | 10. Sweden | 5,6 kg |

The Swiss figure must be adjusted to allow for the number of purchases by tourists (French: 4.3 kg; Spanish, 1.9 kg; Italians, 1.8 kg, etc.).

### The Belgian taste

| | |
|---|---|
| 1. Filled chocolate | 36 % |
| 2. Milk chocolate | 26 % |
| 3. Fondant chocolate | 19 % |
| 4. Hazelnut chocolate | 13 % |
| 5. White chocolate | 5 % |
| 6. Puffed rice chocolate | 1 % |

### Rate of penetration for chocolate

In Belgium chocolate enjoys a national market penetration rate of 83 %; there is no marked difference according to region.

| | |
|---|---|
| - Brussels conurbation | 85 % |
| - Wallonia | 84 % |
| - Flanders | 81 % |

*Wrapping for César chocolate, Antwerp.*

However, analysis by type of finished product shows:
- Fondant chocolate, 41.6 % in Brussels,
- Milk chocolate, 71.6 % in Flanders,
- White and milk chocolate, 46.3 % in Wallonia. (Source: Institut national de statistiques.)

The history of public transport in Brussels, published by the STIB, describes how the vehicles of the commercial railway company (Les Chemins de fer économiques) arrived on the scene in Brussels in 1887. They were known as the "Economiques". Originally they provided 34 open vehicles, and 20 closed ones. Painted brown, with the lower section creamy white, the "Economiques" vehicles were soon known by the popular nickname of "the chocolate trams".

In April 1910 the Solbosch exhibition opened in the area which would later become the Avenue F.-D. Roosevelt and the university. As with earlier exhibitions, it had a centre of popular entertainment, called the "Bruxelles-Kermesse". This recreated - with a certain amount of imagination - some corners of the old city which disappeared when the River Senne was covered over. (In 1958, the Brussels "Expo" would have its "Belgique Joyeuse".)

On the day of the official opening, the Line 33 route was inaugurated (this was the line that figured in Jacques Brel's song *Madeleine* !). To reach the exhibition, visitors could take a Brussels Tramway or an "Economique": regulars simply said "Chocolate !" when they wanted a connecting ticket. The fare rate was set in sections, on a 5-centime base, with a minimum of 10 centimes for second class and 15 centimes in first class. (More than three million visitors took the tram to reach the exhibition between April and August. On 14 August a tragic fire brought the display to a premature close.)

Towards the end of 1913 it was decided to use the same colour for the outside of all vehicles, trams and buses used for public transport in the capital. Henceforward all main units and their secondary following units were painted primrose yellow.

During the eighteenth-century Enlightenment the fashion for chocolate made real advances in Belgium. Charles de Lorraine, Governor-General of the Austrian Netherlands between 1744 and 1780, was a great lover of chocolate and encouraged its consumption.

A register of Court purchases in Brussels records the price of a pound of cocoa: between 35 and 50 sous, a sum which should be related to the wages of an unskilled worker, who would earn around 8 or 9 sous per day ! By this time the manufacturers (the Belgians or Flemish of their day) were already exporting chocolate in blocks stamped with their emblem. The Belgians were the pioneers, for it was not until 1770 that France introduced its first industrial chocolate factory.

Consumption of chocolate as a drink, however, remains low in comparison with coffee or tea. (These three drinks share both their arrival in western Europe in the 16th and 17th centuries and their roots reaching deep into the founding myths of the civilisations which first produced them.) Possession of a set of china for serving chocolate, with a suitable pot, quickly became a sure and acceptable way of emphasising a rise in the social hierarchy. In 1967, in his *Civilisation matérielle et capitalisme*, the distinguished French historian Fernand Braudel writes of the fashion for chocolate at that time: "Great men would sometimes drink it, old people often, the common people never". This was confirmed by Da Ponte, Mozart's librettist, in his opera *Cosi fan Tutte* in 1790, putting into the mouth of the light-hearted Despina the words, "Of chocolate I only taste the aroma. Yes, indeed, it is you who will drink it while I will be happy to watch".

### The 19th Century Age of Pioneers

In 1840 the Berwaerts company announced the sale of chocolate in tablet, drop and figurine forms. A dozen chocolate makers were established during the reign of the first King of the Belgians, Leopold I: they included Meurisse in Antwerp (1845), Delannoy and Joveneaux in Tournai (1847 and 1848), and Neuhaus and Senez-Strubelle in Brussels (1857 and 1860). It was at

## The 20th Century, the Age of Belgian Chocolate

Chocolate production increased at the beginning of the 20th century, and small craftsmen turned to mechanisation. In 1905 Belgium had around fifty chocolate factories, with the most famous making Baron and Martougin brands, both in Antwerp.

As a printed brochure explained at the death of Alfred Martougin in 1952,

It was in 1902 that the young Walloon, rich only in his enthusiasm and determination, settled in Antwerp and set up our chocolate making business and bestowing on it - optimistically for the period, in relation to its size and potential - the description of "model chocolate factory".

By 1910 it could be said that the Belgian chocolate industry was one of the finest in the world. Chocolate became simultaneously democratised and a true consumer product. It became the inescapable and desirable complement to children's food. All classes of the population could afford it, and no longer only the more prosperous elements as in earlier times.

*The Côte d'Or pavilion at the Brussels International and Universal Exhibition, 1935.*

the end of the Rue Neuve, next to the aristocratic chocolate maker Meyers, that Senez-Strubelle had their four shop-windows. Chocolate tablets, or bars, were sold here at 15 centimes each, with a small picture from the "History of Belgium" set. School-children were already collecting and exchanging their patriotic pictures by the end of the nineteenth century. The union of master confectioners was established in 1887; two years later it gave birth in its turn to a "master confectioners' chocolate works".

### Why is Belgian chocolate the best in the world ?

There are five objective reasons which justify the reputation of Belgian chocolate:

1. The excellent quality of the beans used in Belgium. Their origin is selected with care and the processing operations are supervised.

2. Special care is given to the roasting and crushing. (This is taken down to 12 microns, while in Great Britain, for example, the crushing is set at 24 microns.)

3. The quality of the other ingredients, such as the sugar, is similarly superior.

4. The minimum proportion of cocoa solids is 35 per cent, but in practice it is usually 43 per cent.

5. Knowledge and passion are the motivating factors for our small-scale and major craftsmen.

*Chocolate Pot, 1758. (Château de Seneffe, German collection.)*

Chocolate was an ordinary purchase, no longer reserved for certain great occasions such as Easter or Christmas. The selling point for chocolate can be condensed into the expression "optimism".

# The Peaks of Belgian Chocolate

## • Baptista

The Baptista company was founded by Marc Baptista in 1984. Chocolate was selected for its international fame. For a year the infant business carried out trials with a small and carefully selected clientele, in order to establish a range of products. Next, sales were expanded in Brussels and in the provinces. Established in Brussels, in 1992 the company moved into a vast 1600-square-metre hall in the southern suburbs to set up an automatic production line, with a capacity of 15 tonnes per day. The move enabled them to expand their export trade successfully.

Baptista products are basically 70 g and 50 g bars, and a 43 g size inspired by confectionery bars but retaining the properties of true chocolate. Nuggets and pralines are also available, sold in packets or wrapped individually. The company uses non-traditional packaging which enable it to offer unusual and ecological styles.

(Baptista, 52, Chaussée de Nivelles, 1461 Ittre. Tel.: 02/366.02.69. Fax: 02/366.35.39).

## • Barry Callebaut Belgium

In 1850 the five Callebaut brothers founded the industrial "Gebroeders Callebaut" complex at Wieze, each taking responsibility for one speciality: mineral water works, brewery, dairy, flour mill, etc. In 1911 a chocolate-making section was added, which proved so successful that it supplanted all the others.

### A few dates:

1930: foundation of the Callebaut chocolate factory.
1981: take-over by the Swiss firm Interfood.
1983: Klaus J. Jacobs buys Interfood.

Callebaut chocolate wrapper.

1990: Klaus J. Jacobs buys out the British chocolate-coating manufacturer Lesme.
1992: creation of Callebaut Asia Pacific.
1995: founding of the Klaus J. Jacobs Holding group, covering in particular C.J. Van Houten and Callebaut AG.
1996: Klaus J. Jacobs takes back Cacao Barry. Founding of Barry Callebaut. Today, the group consists of 19 production units in Europe, Africa, USA and Asia. This giant group goes on to process 11 per cent of the world cocoa bean production, with estimated sales of 45 billion Belgian francs. The alliance of two leading groups establishes:
• a world leader in client service
• a world leader in fillings and icing paste
• a world leader from cocoa through to chocolate

### Specialities:

Coating chocolate is available in three forms:
1. solid, in blocks of 5 kg - 1 tonne;
2. solid, as small pieces designed

for craft workers, supplied in 2.5 or 10 kg bags;

3. liquid, in tanker-wagons of 10 or 20 tonnes. The liquid form represents 70 per cent of the volume produced.

Barry Callebaut Belgium offers a range of 600 chocolate preparations, a total unequalled in the chocolate industry. Exports represent 70 per cent of its production. *(Barry Callebaut Belgium N.V., 122 Aalstersestraat, 9280 Lebbeke-Wieze. Tel.: 053/73.02.11. Fax: 053/78.04.63).*

## • Belcolade

In 1987 the Puratos company set up Belcolade, which went into production in October of the following year. Established at Aalst-Erembodegem, it offers a "Real chocolate from Belgium" (Belcolade takes pride in being 100 per cent Belgian), a coating chocolate available in liquid form, as chocolate drops, blocks, and fillings based on nuts or fruit, and products such as chocolate chips for chefs and manufacturers. Its network extends across 80 countries. In 1994 Belcolade founded a company in the United States. It produces 20,000 tonnes of chocola-

te and fillings, representing a turnover of 1.8 billion Belgian francs. *(Belcolade, 16, Industrielaan, 9320 Aalst-Erembodegem. Tel.: 053/83.96.00. Fax: 053/83.89.38).*

## • Bruyerre

In 1909 Monsieur Léon-François Bruyerre went into business as a wholesale food materials trader in Gosselies. He soon took over a biscuit factory, which enabled him to extend his trade and to launch out into manufacturing raw materials and equipment for bakers and confectioners, as well as a high-quality range of chocolates and confectionery.

### A few dates

1937: the house of Bruyerre becomes the SPRL Usines Bruyerre, specialising in preserving fruit and the sale of raw materials for the baking and confectionery industry and the manufacture of marzipan and almond paste as well as chocolates and pralines.

1941: Monsieur Léon-François Bruyerre dies and his wife, with the help of their two daughters (married to Monsieur Emile Collet

---

### Nostalgia: the flavour of chocolate, and Tintin

Although the chocolate business was founded in the nineteenth century near the Gare du Nord, for several generations the traveller's point of departure or return (and the daily transit point for commuters) at the Gare du Midi has been synonymous with Côte d'Or chocolate ... and strip-drawn stories ("*bande dessinée*"). Indeed, the illuminated sign with Tintin's head hung out-

*Hergé: illustration for the first edition of Cigares du pharaon (Editions Casterman).*

side the building at the corner of the Place Bara from 1958 onwards (inaugurated by Paul-Henri Spaak and Hergé), long before the excellent introduction of cartoon story tours through Brussels and the opening of the *Bande dessinée* museum. The image was linked with the exotic and persistent aroma filtering out from the Rue Bara chocolate works, pervading all the surrounding streets. Visiting foreigners - Parisians for example - no doubt felt the same as they left their trans-European trains, before the TGV system arrived to modernise the layout of the building along with the whole district. In 1996 Neuhaus introduced Tintin metal boxes containing chocolates with the paper wrappers reproducing illustrations from the famous Hergé albums.

### Training at the Callebaut college

Impressive ! All visitors express the same surprise when they see the premises of the famous Wieze chocolate works near Alost. Among them are "pupils" (praline craftsmen, foreign professionals, etc.) who take free three-day training sessions in which Callebaut specialists teach, in four languages, the art of working chocolate.

### Large-scale Consumption

Three separate threads rule the labours of the firm of Barry Callebaut: large-scale consumption, industry and craftsmen. The production of chocolates for sale to the general public is a return to origins, down to the slogan "Calle-baut, the original". In the words of Jean-Didier Boucau, executive with Callebaut with responsibility for the consumer division: "More than a commercial goal, it is a matter of wishing to remain in contact with the final consumer. This is what enables us to follow his tastes and trends." This is why there are Callebaut bars on food shop shelves (nut chocolate; 50 g Callebaut bars "3 x 4", in the original format with new flavours (caramel, coconut, exotic, moka, 62 per cent cocoa solids, etc.), Callebaut 200 g blocks filled with fruit; vanilla, pistachio, mixed fruit, strawberry, banana and coconut), as well as 100 per cent chocolate granules, with glossy fine grains and entertaining packaging for children. In the last two years, novel-

ties have appeared: "Matinettes" (an ultrafine bar to eat with bread), "Callets Dessert" (chocolate drops with recipes for juvenile cooks), "Choc'idée" (cups and decorations), "Classics" (individually wrapped mini-bars).

### Barry Callebaut and Industry

"More than 80 per cent of our turnover comes from the chocolate industries, including 70 per cent for export," explains Pierre Vermout, Managing Director of Barry Callebaut. Callebaut offers its customers 600 recipes - that does not mean the same number of different flavours, for the variety of recipes also depends on other factors, such as viscosity. The service is comprehensive, and the quality constant. In this respect, products are tested very regularly, with teams checking them for taste: sweet, bitter-sweet, refreshing, fruit, etc., and factors such as roasting, chemistry, oxidation, etc.

The test chamber next to the computerised laboratory is in itself a surprise in the tour of the Barry Callebaut premises. If there is the slightest hesitation, a team of testers is brought together and put to work. Decisions are taken not by a majority but by consensus: there must be full agreement among the determined testers. Further, a team of researchers is engaged in looking for new uses for chocolate (iced chocolate, new specialities, the association between biscuit and chocolate, etc.). Three-quarters of industrial chocolate is delivered in liquid form. The tanker lorries are filled with a wealth of precautions (matching the standard throughout the factory). Chocolate is delivered in liquid form, in containers. In this case, they can be left on site for two or three weeks. The remainder of chocolate comes in

*The Callebaut factory at Wieze, early 20th century.*

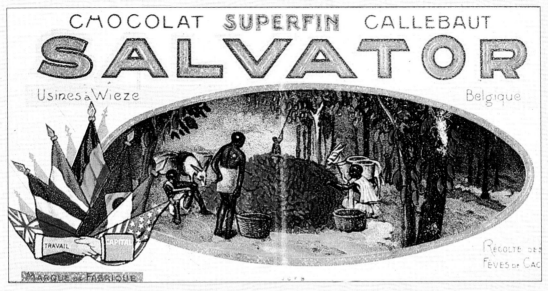

CHOCOLAT SUPERFIN CALLEBAUT
SALVATOR
Usines à Wieze                    Belgique

TRAVAIL    CAPITAL

MARQUE DE FABRIQUE

RÉCOLTE DES
FÈVES DE CAC

*Wrapper for the Salvator chocolate baton which introduced Callebaut chocolate.*

small pieces, "Callets", which can even be worked in micro-wave ovens, or in 5-kg blocks. Professionals ask for Type 811 chocolate when they want "bitter chocolate with a full-bodied flavour" or Type W11 for "very sweet white chocolate" - a language for the initiated, which always amuses outsiders.

### Barry Callebaut and craftsman chocolate workers

Skill in chocolate-making is not only represented by small-scale praline makers, bakers and confectioners - it is also to be found in hotels, restaurants, cafés and tea-rooms. In effect, the Callebaut brand plays its part right through to chocolate desserts or chocolate ice-creams, for

an impressive number of grand tables or in the major brands. Häagen-Dazs and the Ledoyen restaurant in Paris are examples - but there are also all the great gastronomic names throughout the world (where Callebaut is a true ambassador for our high-quality chocolate), and at home, since Comme Chez Soi, La Villa Lorraine and Chez Bruneau are enthusiastic customers of Callebaut. The famous Callebaut school is open to these chocolate specialists and their staff, for a better understanding of chocolate and how best to use it in all its guises. Guide-books are also published for their guidance, with recipes for confectionery and brioches as well as for sauces, decoration or pralines. Then there is a strip-drawn story

retracing the history of the Callebaut family, and giving clear explanations on how chocolate is made - the "laminage" (flattening) for example, which refines the chocolate paste by crushing it between cylinders which are adjusted closer and closer together, to reduce the powder to an extremely fine texture. This super-fine pressing is one of the reasons for the superior quality of Belgian chocolate.

the help of their two daughters (married to Monsieur Emile Collet and Monsieur Maurice Collet) take over his work. During the Second World War the business has to halt its activities, and start up operations again later. In order to concentrate the investment, the only activities continued are the production of luxury pralines and trade in raw materials, and machinery and chilling equipment for bakery and confectionery. 1980: the SPRL becomes a limited company, when the third generation of the Bruyerre Collet company takes up the torch.

1987: the Usines Bruyerre company divides into four separate limited companies headed by a financial and property holding company: Usines Bruyerre SA, Belgram Equipment SA, Bruyerre Equip'Tout SA and Le Chocolatier Bruyerre SA.

1992 Death of Monsieur Thierry Collet, who introduced special products into Great Britain, France, Japan and North America. His wife, Fabiola Collet, works as Managing Director in close collaboration with Jean-Pierre Collet, the Managing Director of the Groupe Bruyerre.

Today, the annual production stands at 150 tonnes of pralines, representing more than 75 types. The early spirit survives, for only the finest ingredients are used, and many products are still finished by hand. The Chocolatier Bruyerre is one of the few Belgian chocolate manufacturers which still makes its own fillings - for example, the company still roasts its own hazelnuts, which are imported from Turkey.

"In an economic context," states Thierry Schamp, sales manager, "where the production of food products moves increasingly towards mass production, the infinite variety of chocolate still enables the craftsman to express his talents to the full, within the purest Belgian tradition".

*(Le Chocolatier Bruyerre, S.A.*
*47, Chaussée de Bruxelles,*
*6041 Gosselies. Tel.: 071/85.22.42*
*Fax: 071/85.33.38).*

## • *Cacao Goemaere*

Established in Drongen (Ghent) since 1888, it makes coating chocolate. After 85 years as a family concern, the company was bought in 1973 by the French group Cacao Barry (founded in 1842), which has a dozen factories throughout the world. (The Belgian Albert Frère has owned 49 per cent of the group's component elements since 1994). Its turnover exceeds 3 billion Belgian francs annually. Michel Goemare, the general manager, considers that the company successfully combines the advantages of a multinational with those of a small or medium-size company. In 1996 Cacao Barry was acquired by Klaus Jacobs, and became Barry Callebaut.

*(Cacao Goemaere, 6, Industriege-*
*bied Drongen-Booiebos,*
*9031 Drongen. Tel.: 09/282.55.11.*
*Fax: 09/282.63.99).*

## • *Chocolaterie Guylian*

The company was founded in 1967 following the marriage of Guy and Liliane Foubert, hence the name "Guylian", the combination of their first names. Guy Foubert, one of nine children, grew up in his parents' bakery and enrolled at the Antwerp school of confectionery and patisserie, where he developed an innate talent for making high-quality pralines. He began his career by selling "home made" truffles in the local market. In 1988, Guylian moved into entirely new premises at Sint-Niklaas, some twenty kilometres from Antwerp. When Guy Foubert died in 1986, his daughter Dominique, then a 22-year-old student in England, took over the business as manager. Her husband developed the marketing side and the image of Guylian, concentrating particularly on large-scale distribution and duty-free sales throughout the world.

**Specialities:**

Chocolate *Fruits de Mer*: filled with Guylian hazelnut praline, they are appreciated everywhere in the world. The ingredients are selected from West Africa's finest cocoa beans and the plumpest Mediterranean hazelnuts.

This amazing Guylian speciality consists of eleven marbled shapes of tempting elegance. Today these exquisite chocolate creations are an essential part of the international chocolate trade, and the company employs a wide range of packaging to meet all the requirements of the retail trade.

## Guylian: the famous chocolate Fruits de Mer

Guy and Liliane Foubert began making their chocolate truffles in 1960. Because they were sold principally in winter, they wished to find an equivalent for the spring and summer. And why not *Fruits de Mer* made of chocolate? Guy Foubert was the first to adapt modern technology to make his famous fruits de mer in large quantities. Today, in the Sint-Niklaas factory (covering more than 25,000 square metres), and despite highly sophisticated production techniques, the original recipe developed by Guy Foubert in 1958 has not changed. The production line is highly automated and manufacturing secrets are closely protected.

### An original recipe

What is the secret that makes this product unique in its field? For a recipe to succeed, it must obviously use ingredients of the highest quality. The basis of the chocolate is a blend of the best cocoa beans from West Africa, a region in which Belgium has gained an international reputation for quality. The hazelnuts come from the finest growing areas of the Mediterranean basin. They are very carefully selected for the size and quality which will guarantee the Guylian flavour. They are roasted and caramelised in traditional copper cauldrons. At this stage of production, the experience of the master chocolatier is crucial in judging the degree of caramelisation. Once this operation is finished, the nuts are crushed and added to the preparation of a fine paste. Then they need only the chocolate to obtain the famous praline.

Guylian uses three kinds of chocolate, milk, dark and white, and it is the blend of the three materials which produces the famous marbled effect of Guylian Fruits de Mer.

### An artistic creation

Guylian *Fruits de Mer* make up an unique collection in their field and are the work of a fine artist. Each shape has been minutely observed, designed and sculpted in potter's clay from which the plaster cast is made for the manufacturing mould. The Guylian collection consists of eleven different shapes. Each chocolate sweet, poured into a carefully designed mould, includes the letter "G"; this stamp enables consumers throughout the whole world to be sure of the origin of Guylian *Fruits de Mer*
Bringing together art and tradition, these Guylian creations occupy a distinguished place among the finest Belgian chocolates.

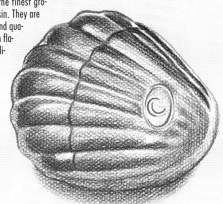

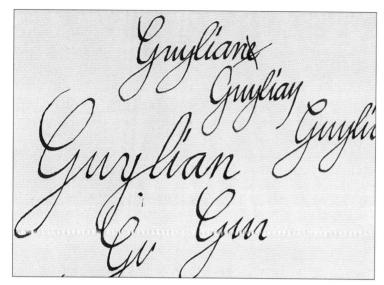

1996, Les Poussins du P'tit Guy and La Canasta.

Guylian products are sold in more than 140 countries. The manufacturing unit in Sint-Niklaas is constantly expanding, and its complete automation enables it to produce more than 75 tonnes of chocolates each day. Guylian is a leader in the sector of boxed Belgian chocolates as well as in the international duty free markets. The Guylian chocolate *Fruits de Mer* are among the five best sellers. Guylian does not have its own outlets; all retail sales are through major stores throughout the world, and in confectionery and praline shops, bakeries, etc.

Sales of the chocolate *Fruits de Mer* grow steadily and for this reason the company regularly brings up to date the packaging which have contributed to Guylian's fame.

The range of packaging and transport arrangements offers an answer to all requirements and sales of all kinds.

*(Chocolaterie Guylian, 1, Europark-Oost, 9100 Saint-Niklaas.*
*Tel.: 03/760.97.00.*
*Fax: 03/777.06.81).*

Guylian owes its reputation as a leader in the international chocolate market not only to the steadily growing success of the chocolate *Fruits de Mer* but also to its creation of new product lines.

La Trufflina: in 1992 Guylian launched a new kind of praline truffle, La Trufflina, prepared from Guy and Liliane's recipes. La Trufflina takes its inspiration from a love story set against the background of 16th century Venetian extravagance. It began when a rich confectioner fell madly in love with a noble Venetian lady.

The love-lorn confectioner paid court to her with offers of what he did best: his pralines. The selection of milk, fondant and white chocolate for La Trufflina reflects the changing nature of its inspiration. The creamy filling for the truffle is lovingly coated with chocolate and covered with delicious flakes of extra-fine chocolate; complete, it is prettily presented in a delicate pleated ruff.

Opus: encouraged by the success of La Trufflina, Guylian extended the range of products with Opus in 1995 and La Perlina in

GUYLIAN

III. Belgian chocolate makers

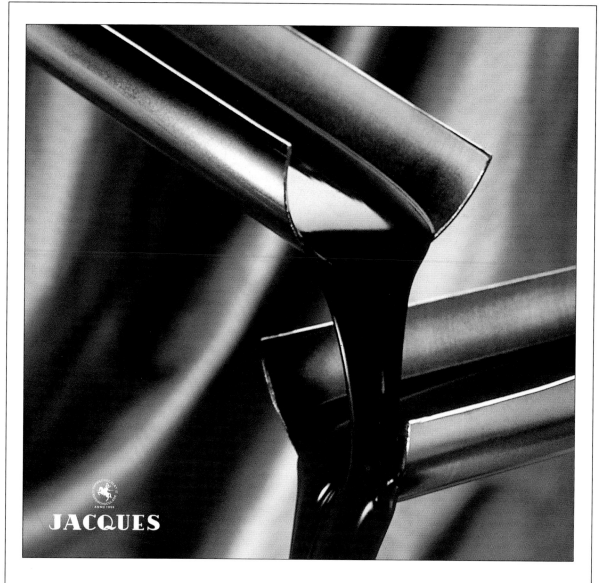

Belgian chocolate

## • Chocolaterie Jacques

The company was founded in 1890 by Jean-Antoine Jacques, son of a Louveigné farmer: he started his career by creating the "Le Semeur" brand. The brand which bears his name was officially launched in 1896. After its association with a group of industrialists in Verviers in 1920 and its establishment in Eupen in 1923, the chocolate manufacturing business expanded very rapidly. In 1982 it joined the German group Stollwerck-Sprengel. The year 1987 brought the opening of a new production unit, which won the Wallonia prize for exports in 1993.

Jacques produces coating chocolate and a range of classics for specific clients: 50 g batons, 200 g bars, and 400 g packets of napolitains. Today, 250 people work in the chocolate factory producing annual sales of 25,000 tonnes, 79 per cent of which is exported to 25 different countries. Since 1994 Jacques has promoted its "Royaume du Chocolat" ("Chocolate Kingdom"), consisting of a tour of the factory,

*Founder's share certificate for the Chocolaterie Jacques at Verviers (Eupen, Chocolaterie Jacques museum).*

the permanent museum and a "Chocolate Space". (Tel. for tours: 087/59.29. 67).
*(Chocolaterie Jacques,*
*16, Industriestrasse, 4700 Eupen.*
*Tel.: 087/59.29.11.*
*Fax: 087/59.29.29).*

## • Cocachoc

The Cocachoc company was founded in 1979 and has come to specialise in chocolate and bisuits. This family business, with M. Marcel Caeyers as its General Sales Manager, manufactures and distributes goods in two sectors: traditional food stores - department stores, discount stores, supermarkets, Cash & Carry shops, wholesalers - and hotels, restaurants and catering establishments. In 1989 Cocachoc's turnover was 90 million Belgian francs, with twenty employees, while in 1997 it stands at 370 million BF, with 32 employees.

Cocachoc produces truffles with milk chocolate flakes, nuggets of grated coconut coated in fondant chocolate with various flavours (rum, coffee, strawberry, banana), and confectionery bars (Bouchée coco). All these products are sold at supermarket tills, in duty-free shops, confectioners, petrol stations and the confectionery shelves in department stores.

Cocachoc also offers seasonal products and hollow chocolate goods. Coloured boxes containing seven figures, weighing 100 g, are made in two kinds of chocolate: the upper part of white chocolate and the lower part of milk chocolate. The back of the

## The colour-print venture

The expression "chromo" (colour print), is derived from "chromolithography". It is used dismissively, to indicate a poor quality colour reproduction, but that was the name used from the end of the 19th century for the little pictures which were put inside chocolate bar wrappers. The Chocolaterie Jacques was an example of this enthusiasm. In 1905 they launched a series when they created the "Le Semeur" brand of chocolate. The back of the wrapping bore the message: "I have the pleasure of presenting to my many customers an attractive collection of 126 different chromos, with a print inside each package of "Le Semeur" chocolate. Anyone who sends in a complete collection in the "Semeur" album (price 1 franc from my stockists) will receive in return a prize of 12 francs in chocolate."

The pictures show gypsies, exotic birds, plantations of cocoa, tea or coffee, coins, elephants, etc.

Shortly after its establishment as a limited company, the Jacques chocolate company distributed little colour-prints designed to be collected in small albums, size 21 x 18 cm. These depicted inventions, various nations, historic facts, games, etc.

### Football Glory

In March 1931 the Jacques chocolate baton appeared for the first time in

the form that still exists today. Although bars contained postcards, this was also the period when small pictures and photographs were first slipped into wrappings. Like other manufacturers, Jacques created the "Champion" and "Ideal Star" brands containing photographs of artists or stars in other areas. The "Goal" brand contained a photograph of a footballer, designed to fit an album with space for 120 pictures.

The "Chevalier Jacques" first appeared in October 1937. The following year, the attachment of the Belgian nation to their King Léopold III and Queen Astrid inspired a series of pictures showing the royal family. The first series was followed in 1939 by a second distribution, each containing 96 colour-prints.

The years 1939-40 witnessed one of the finest Jacques series: "Cars, aircraft and warships", a set of 360 small colour-prints and 18 large ones, illustrating the various styles in these categories. The tragic events of those years was sadly to interrupt the distribution for many collectors, leaving many of the albums with empty spaces for ever.

The wide range of album titles which have been issued since 1945 includes: "Retrospective on locomotives" (1952), "In search of the stars" (1963), "The Geography of Belgium" (1970), etc.

*The Chevalier Jacques.*

A distinctive collection consisted of the pictures "Quick et Flupke" in 1985 and 1988, designed to be stuck in an album or on a calendar.

### Le Petit Spirou

Today, after 100 years of existence, the Chocolaterie Jacques chooses to go back in time, relaunching and bring up to date these colour prints which were its glory. They are slipped into the wrapping of three new varieties of chocolate (Twinko, Kiko and Krako), 24 new images to be collected and stuck into a booklet under the title "The Secret of the Baton". The star of these pictures is Le Petit Spirou, the character created by André Franquin and continued by Tome et Janry.

carton can be coloured in by children. This product is also available in individual packets - Samson (in the shape of a dog), Charly Duck (a duck), Surprise (St Nicolas) and Merry Christmas (Father Christmas).

The company also specialises in making chocolate truffles in individual packages of 5 g, 7.5 g and 10 g, which are sold through wholesalers and firms supplying the hotel, restaurant and café trade. In the "catering" sector, the products are served with a cup of coffee or tea. They are available under the Cocachoc label or with the customer's name.

Two new products are available:
- a milk chocolate baton at 100 g, 50 g or 30 g, made of fine nougat, almonds and honey. This is also available in boxes of 24 or 60.
- a butter biscuit with milk or dark chocolate, 125 g, or in boxes containing 16 biscuits.

Cocachoc exports 55 per cent of its merchandise, under the direction of export manager M. Roger Hamblok. The chief buying coun-

tries are the Netherlands, France, Japan, Germany, Denmark, Ireland, Spain, Italy, Finland, Austria, South Africa, Russia, the U.S.A., and Canada.
(*Cocachoc, 49, Toekomstlaan, 2200 Herentals.*
*Tel.: 014/25.96.00.*
*Fax: 014/22.44.43).*

## • *Confiserie Léonidas*

Léonidas Kestekidès settled in the United States at the beginning of the 20th century. As a member of the Greek delegation from the USA, he attended first the Brussels World Exhibition in 1910 and then the Universal

*Léonidas Kestekidès, founder of Léonidas*

Exhibition at Ghent in 1913. He fell in love with a beautiful Brussels girl, married her, and decided to settle in Belgium. He opened shops in Brussels, Blankenberghe and Ghent. His success was immediate, with tremendous sales which continue to grow and now include the finest quality praline at the best prices, for a product which is the most famous in the world for its freshness.

**A few dates:**
1913: Foundation in Ghent
1935: Basile Kestekidès takes over the company and establishes a shop in the Boulevard Anspach, Brussels
1970: the company changes its status from SPRL to become a limited company
1983: in addition to the factory in the Rempart des Moines, at the heart of Brussels, a second factory is established in the Boulevard Graindor at Anderlecht
1993: foundation of a third factory, in the Rue Prévinaire, Anderlecht
Léonidas has 1750 sales points throughout the world. New York

City, Chicago, Atlanta, Bahrein, Kuweit, Warsaw, Gdansk, Bergamo, San Sebastian, Palma de Mallorca, Athens, Cologne, Berlin, Frankfort, etc... The turnover in 1995 was 3 billion Belgian francs, and Léonidas produces two-thirds of all Belgian pralines.

**Specialities:**
More than 83 types of praline, always sold individually.
Inventions between 1980 and 1995: "Casanova" praline, "Carré croquant" with puffed rice, "Tutti-Frutti" with white chocolate, etc. "Manon Léonidas": Léonidas has replaced the fondant sugar of the classic manon with a coating of white chocolate, and the walnut with a toasted hazelnut.
*(Confiserie Léonidas, 43, boulevard J.-Graindor, 1070 Brussels.*
*Tel.: 02/522.19.57.*
*Fax: 02/522.09.43).*

## • Côte d'Or

In 1870, Charles Neuhaus sets up a chocolate factory in the Rue des Palais in Schaerbeek. In 1998 Joseph Bieswal, a native of Furnes, buys the company.
In 1895 he sells the building to Lambert Michiels, a confectioner in Tirlemont, and settles in another, more modern, building in the Rue des Palais. Both, however, have to leave their premises in 1899 after compulsory purchase for the construction of the Nord station. Bieswal and Michiels settle together in a former mill in the

Rue Bara at Anderlecht. In 1906 they combine to form the Alimenta company.

**A few dates:**
1883: registration of the "Côte d'Or" brand
1906: creation of the Alimenta company. First appearance of the logo and the elephant
1911: Alimenta becomes a cooperative. Launch of the chocolate packet in its famous white and gold paper
1929: Victor Michiels becomes chairman after the death of Lambert Michiels (1923) and of Joseph Bieswal (1929)
1935: participation in the Brussels Universal Exhibition.
1940-46: Congobar replaces Côte d'Or
1958: participation in the Brussels Universal Exhibition
1961: Jean Michiels takes over as chairman on the death of Constant-Victor Michiels
1964: creation of the Côte d'Or company
1972: Jean Michiels retires from business and Paul Bieswal becomes chairman. Creation of Côte d'Or France and Côte d'Or Nederland

1974: construction of the Seclin factory

1975: Vincent Bieswal is named chairman

1977: Baudouin Michiels takes over the chairmanship. Establishment of a warehouse in Halle

1978: creation of Côte d'Or in Switzerland and Great Britain

1982: creation of the Côte d'Or Company of America

1983: celebration of the firm's centenary

1984: the shares are quoted on the stock exchange

1985-86: sponsorship of Eric Tabarly's yacht Côte d'Or 1987: take-over by the Jacobs Suchard group

1989: foundation of Jacobs Suchard-Côte d'Or

1990: Jacobs Suchard is itself absorbed by the American group Philip Morris, with the exception of Callebaut and Van Houten. Acquisition of the ISO certificate (a world-wide system of quality control), a first for a Belgian food company, a first for a chocolate firm at world level

1993: within the American group, fusion of Jacobs-Suchard

## Pierre Iserantant, our finest craftsman

All the specialists in the business are in agreement: Pierre Iserentant is their finest craftsman... and yet he remains unknown to the general public. The reason is a simple one: his product is always "reprocessed" before it is available to the consumer. Only the professionals do business with him. This book is therefore the ideal place to pay homage to him.

'Pierre Iserentant naturally makes no concessions when it is a matter of the quality of raw materials or the finished product. Further, he shows a rigour unknown anywhere else in the world', say the nation's greatest chocolate makers.

*Pierre Iserentant.*

We offer here descriptions of some of his products, made entirely of chocolate, and which are truly mouth-watering: 'Marie-José' is a cup bought by confectioners, who fill it with a small piece of sponge cake, Kirsch, fruit, and fresh cream. It's divine ! There is a variation called the `Marie-Annette'.

The `Snobinette' is a mini-cup bought by great restaurants, who fill it with praline or a fresh cream and serve it with coffee. The "Cigarette" is a fine layer of chocolate rolled up like a cigarette - a delicate art ! It is used by confectioners or ice-cream makers as a decoration. "Chips" are used to surround gâteaux, truffles, etc.

Pierre Iserentant has worked with seven people since 1970. He exports around 60 per cent of his production. One of his secrets: he does not work with moulds, but by dipping. The work is therefore done entirely outside the mould, producing a little roundness at the base of the chocolate, and its hand-made appearance.

"Some people are passionate about the flavour or the aroma of the chocolate, I am more devoted to the technique of making it. I have spent my life developing my own ways of making it. I am not an engineer, to be precise I am ingenious ..." says our finest craftsman. Pierre Iserentant, 28 rue de Battice, 4800 Petit-Rechain. Tel.: 087/33.94.64.

and Kraft General Food. Birth of Kraft Jacobs Suchard-Côte d'Or (Halle, Herentals and Liège) and Kraft Jacobs Suchard (Namur). Winning of the important "Export Oscar"

1994: the prime minister inaugurates the chocolate factory at Halle (an investment of two billion Belgian franc)

1995: integration of the Netherlands into the new Benelux commercial structure

1996: birth of Kraft Jacobs Suchard, with Baudouin Michiels as chairman

### The Origin of the name "Côte d'Or"

If the stamps stuck on the envelopes of the bills and delivery notes had not been so handsome, the "Côte d'Or" brand would probably not have adopted the elephant. In fact the great grandfather of Baudouin Michiels, the current chairman of the company, was so impressed at the end of the 19th century by postage stamps from the Gold Coast that he promptly decided to use the elephant as an image for his chocolate. These coloured stamps showed a pyramid, a palm tree and an elephant, all of them exotic characteristics for this mythic and magical food substance. He even gave up the brand in his own name, "Michiels", to adopt "Côte d'Or".

Before 1873 the Portuguese called it `El Mina'; following its independence on 6 March 1957, the "Gold Coast" became Ghana, a republic which is still a member of the Commonwealth. The capital, Accra, now has more than 15 million inhabitants. Ghana lies next to the Ivory Coast; it is the largest cocoa exporter in the world, with a turnover of 225 billion CFA francs in 1990.

A footnote to history: the elephant, symbol of power and the exotic, has had only three different representations in the whole history of the company.

### The Temple of Chocolate

For a month, Antoine had been passionate about chocolate. Of course he is a little greedy and like all children of his age (he has just had his 10th birthday !), his mother lets him buy a chocolate baton at play-time, but he was ignorant of a great many facts about his favourite sweet. Where do cocoa trees grow? Is the tube of cocoa butter which is used in winter the same as in chocolate? Does chocolate cause tooth decay?

*Anniversary souvenir box from the World Fair, for Côte d'Or chocolate, 1985.*

All these questions come together in class and the teacher answers them, with the help of a "teaching dossier" given to him by the Côte d'Or company in order to prepare for the visit to the "Temple of Chocolate" !

### The Traveller's Diary

In his notebook (checked by his teacher), Antoine has decided to narrate his adventure; rather like ships' captains recorded their travels:

*"... A coach took us to the entrance of the majestic Temple of Chocolate. We waited in a large room where all at once a pirate, a sailor, appeared and welcomed us. He offered us a journey through time ! The first room we went into was a Toltecan temple. He told us the legend of the chocolate king, Quetzalcoatl, while on the walls frescoes illustrated the legend and in the display cases real objects were lit up one at a time ..."*

*The elephant: symbol of the Côte d'Or company since the end of the 19th century.*

4 petits au goût grand comme ça.

MINI-TABLETTES

*Côte d'Or: a great brand which "creates little ones".*

Then, along a passage which moved through time: important dates on the walls, and underfoot a kind of clock mechanism which indicated the passing of time ...

*"... We were inside the hull of a Spanish galleon .. which moved, with the waves ! The wooden deck vibrated, you could hear the wind, and sacks of cocoa beans were piled up in a corner next to a chest full of gold and diamonds ..."*

In the old factory from the beginning of the century, the sailor-narrator explained the harvest and how chocolate is made. And finally ...

*"It's fabulous ! I had some liquid chocolate in a tempering machine and I poured it into little moulds. I made my own chocolate ! And I was able to colour in the wrapper ... I drew ... an elephant !"*

The tour, which lasts about two hours, ends with a visit to two production lines in the very new Côte d'Or factory .. and with a packet made entirely of chocolate ! Antoine ends his tale, *All my life, I'll remember this visit to the Temple of Chocolate !*

## A Universal Response

At the inauguration of the Temple of Chocolate, Philippe Vander Putten, the Managing Director, said, 'Clearly this project responds to a need. It is our way of answering everything that everyone has always wanted to know about cho-

colate, or relating to it, but which no one has ever, or rarely, been able to bring to life in an an active way.'

Active this visit certainly is. It is the starting point for the realisation of the Euroculture company ("Tout Hergé", "Tout Simenon" and "I was 20 in 1945"), a voyage through history, design and objects which illustrate the Belgian cultural heritage. The success is such that we have been forced to double the number of daily tours, from two to four.

We should recall that these visits are designed for primary school pupils, limited to 50 pupils per group. (Reservations: 02/362.38.92) To date, more than 40,000 young people have undertaken this indulgent visit!

*Children discovering the Temple of Chocolate (Côte d'Or).*

**A Brief History of Specialities:**

1935: creation of the "Crèmes" bars, of "Un Dessert" (the first praline baton), and of "Mignonettes"

1937: creation of the "bouchée" and of the "Double lait" milk chocolat baton

1946: launch of "Codorettes"

1948: creation of "rafraîchissants" and "Menthe" toffees

1950: launch of "Chokotoff" chocolate caramels

1951: creation of "Croquettant"

1955: launch of the "Nougatti" bouchée

1958: launch of small 150 g packets

1959: creation of "Cherries"

1960: launch of "Pastador" and creation of whole hazelnut blocks

1962: launch of "crème liquide" bars

1970: creation of the "Kriffi" bouchée

1975: launch of the "Zouki" and "Fli-Fli"

1980: new "Pastador" line

1981: launch of "Bonbon-bloc croquant"

1982: launch of "Mini" pieces, "Cool" batons and 100-g "Blocs noisettes entières" (whole hazelnut bars)

1983: creation of "Cool 4 fruits" batons

1995: "Snax"

1996: "Mini tablettes"

**The Company**

The history of Côte d'Or is a great and attractive adventure. It began in 1883, but when in 1906 the two chocolate makers Bieswal and Michiels combined to form the Alimenta company and decided to adopt the elephant, this was to remain the symbol and mascot of their brand. It added an exotic touch - but more than that, it evoked power, strength, loyalty, perseverance and longevity. From the Rue des Palais in Brussels to the most modern of today's factories, set up in 1995 in Halle, it can be said that the logo has brought good fortune. One of the keys of the brand's success is its direct contact with the consumer. An example is the presence of Côte d'Or in a pavilion beside Lake Hostade (Malines) in 1930, a prelude to its participation at the great exhibitions (and the creation of new products, also linked to the exhibitions: "Mignonettes" in 1935 and "Dessert" in 1958), to the opening of the factory (during the 1960s and '70s, Côte d'Or organised school visits to its factory in the Rue Bara) and finally of the "Temple du Chocolat", which is its logical sequel. Although it was always used, particularly on packaging and in some PR communications, in 1996 the Côte d'Or elephant returned to its origins. Advertising displayed the pachyderm and its young ones on 36-square metre posters as well as in two films shot in Botswana. They showed a consumer carried away by the intense flavour of a chocolate baton and the land disappearing beneath his feet. The elephant appears to take him up and rescue him.

*(Côte d'Or Kraft Jacobs Suchard, 450, Brusselsesteenweg, 1500 Halle. Tel: 02/362.31.11. Fax: 02/362.38.40).*

## • *Galler Chocolatiers*

Jean Galler, apprenticed to his baker-confectioner father, undertook his final training at the Basle school of confectionery in Switzerland. He was proclaimed the "Best Belgian Apprentice" by the federation of bakers and confectioners. In 1975 he spent a period with Lenôtre in Paris. Fascinated by chocolate, he bought the former Clovis chocolate works and at the age of 21, with his father Pierre Galler, he founded a company at Vaux-Sous-Chèvremont in 1976.

### A few dates:

1976: creation of the Galler company
1993: launch of 100 g bars: "Espèces en voie d'apparition"
1994, June: launch of "Nouveaux tartinables", four spreading pastes

---

### Philippe Geluck offers his "tongue" to the "cat"

Jean Galler rang me one day and asked whether the name "*langue de chat*" reminded me of anything. I said that it made me think of my childhood but that it's almost impossible to find these long flat little chocolates, rounded at each end. (In fact, the *langue de chat*, or "cat's tongue", is made of chocolate in Switzerland and in Belgium, while in France it is a biscuit.) "That's right", he said, "I am a chocolate maker and you draw *Le Chat*, the cat. Wouldn't it be a good idea to relaunch the product?" I thought it was an excellent idea. We met initially, taking advantage of our participation in the team for "Le Jeu des dictionnaires" during the "Crystal Antenna" awards in Liège - and we got on very well ! When I returned home I immediately sketched a few ideas and faxed them to him. It already looked like the final result. We remained in contact for several years (he sent me chocolates, I had copies of my books sent to him), and then the time came when it seemed right to set up the project. For another two years we discussed the choice of chocolate, the best flavour, the presen-

*Philippe Geluck: advertisement for Les Langues de Chat. (Galler, 1995)*

tation and the design which would evoke a tin of cat food but which would be opened without using a tin-opener, to avoid injuring children .. I undertook technical research over the shape of the head: we went through queries, it was cut down in size, lightened ... It was fascinating ! All the time, I was discovering a new world, for example the manufacturer of the Gembloux boxes, whose factory I visited.

Today, I am delighted with this product and proud of it; it combines visual and gastronomic qualities. I can say that because I am only one link in the chain of its creation. When I am asked if I liked chocolate before these *langues de chat*, I quote my parents who said, "He would sell his soul to the devil for a bit of chocolate". Now, I have signed a pact with a devil of a man, Jean Galler !
(Philippe Geluck publishes the "Le Chat" albums: *Le Chat, Le Retour du Chat, La Vengeance du Chat*, etc., as well as general encyclopaedias: *Un peu de tout, Made in Belgium*, and *Le Docteur G*, all published by Editions Casterman.)

---

1994: Jean Galler is honoured by King Albert II with the title of Supplier to the Court
1995, January: Jean Galler is elected "Manager of the Year" by the magazine *Trends Tendances*

1995, April: opening in the Grand-Place, Brussels, of a sales outlet, the first to follow the shop at Vaux-sous-Chèvremont, shortly followed by a third in the Rue du Pot-d'Or in Liège

1995: launch of "Langues de Chat" with Philippe Geluck

**Specialities:**
The 70-g chocolate bar. From 1993, a range of six 100-g bars under the name "Espèces en voie d'apparition".

Since 1993 the Galler company's turnover is 250 million Belgian francs. 15 per cent comes from exports: the United States, Australia, the Philippines, Puerto-Rico, Germany, etc.

The chocolates are on sale at more than 2,000 outlets in Belgium and throughout the world. "The" Belgian chocolate by Galler can be seen in certain prestigious showcases, such as the luxury boutique at Amman airport in Jordan, the grand department store Harrods in London, or the Grande Epicerie Fine in Paris. The craft element (decoration, shapes, cartons, shops, etc.) is in the hands of Jean Galler's wife Yvette.
*(Galler Chocolateries, 39, rue de la Station, 4051 Chaudfontaine. Tel.: 04/367.22.11. Fax: 04/365.92.20).*

## • *Godiva*

During the 1920s, Pierre Draps founded a chocolate and confectionery business in Brussels, supplying the large shops, which sold his pralines under their own label. His son Joseph (who worked alongside his father from the age of 14) soon showed his own consi-

derable creative skills. As a master chocolatier, he invented combinations of delicate flavours. Nor did his commercial thinking lag behind. In 1946, with his wife Gabrielle, he founded the firm of Godiva, determined to turn his pralines into a luxury product and to give them international distribution.

**A few dates:**
1946: foundation of "Godiva" in Brussels
1958: opening of a shop in the Rue Saint-Honoré in Paris
1966: opening of a shop on 5th Avenue, New York
1968: Godiva receives its warrant as supplying to the Belgian Court
1974: the firm comes under the aegis of the Campbell's Soup Company to pursue its strategy of international expansion. Two production units work for Godiva, one in Brussels, the other in Pennsylvania, in the United States
1988: Godiva is the official chocolate at the Seoul Olympic Games
1997: Hong Kong, Singapore, Japan, the United Arab Emirates and Kuweit are now regularly sup-

plied by air with super-fresh pralines prepared in Brussels

Four distribution channels are used for the chocolate:
- the firm's own shops
- franchises
- shops-within-a-shop, as in Saks and Bloomingdales in the United States, Harrods in London or KDW in Berlin
- duty free shops in the world's principal airports
Godiva records a turnover of 1 billion Belgian francs, of which exports represent 60 per cent.

### Specialities:
Praline, always their own manufacture, is the basis of Godiva's reputation, as is the sophisticated recipe for its pralines. (The recipe book, with its 70-odd basic specialities created by Joseph Draps, is carefully kept under lock and key.) The manons are always made by hand in traditional fashion: the marzipan base, the gently prepared fresh cream with a nut on top are then dipped in fondant sugar at the precise temperature required. The "Autant", created to mark the Brussels opening of the film "Gone

with the Wind" (in French, *Autant en emporte le vent*), is a house classic. It consists of a shell of dark chocolate filled with chocolate cream with cognac and coffee cream, then coated with milk chocolate. The decoration, a flake of dark chocolate, is hand-prepared. Novelty: Godiva offers a version of "Autant" with a white chocolate coating.

Godiva is also famous for its seasonal chocolates, in accord with its collections of sophisticated packaging, which make very stylish gifts appreciated throughout the world. For each festival (Saint-Nicolas, Christmas, Valentine's Day, Easter), the Godiva master-chocolatier invents new pralines (some thirty each year) and magnificent craftsman-made chocolate creations.
*(Godiva, 5, rue de l'Armistice, 1081 Brussels.*
*Tel.: 02.422.17.11.*
*Fax: 02/422.17.00).*

## • *Kathy Chocolaterie*
In 1919 August Verheecke opened a pâtisserie on the outskirts of Bruges. Four years later, the esta-

### The legend of Lady Godiva
It happened in England in the 11th century. In 1057, in Coventry, Leofric, Count of Chester and husband of Lady Godiva, taxed the poor with unreasonable severity despite the pleas of his wife. Exasperated by her persistence, the husband, knowing her to be shy and modest, issued a challenge which he thought she would never accept: to cross the city on horseback, completely naked. She took up the challenge. Swiftly the whole city learned what was happening and, in order not to embarrass the lady who was sacrificing herself for them, chose to stay indoors when the time came. And so Lady Godiva, dressed only in her long fair hair, crossed a deserted city ... to the great rage of her boorish husband. It is said that a single inhabitant had a look at the beautiful lady and excused himself: "It was so long since I saw a white horse ...!" Today a statue immortalises the scene in the city of Coventry, and in acknowledgement of the "Godiva" brand, Joseph Draps has been honoured with the title of "Freeman of the City".

Lady Godiva, on the famous
praline maker's logo.

blishment had outgrown its premises and moved to Katelijnestraat and then to Groeningen. His son, Georges Verheecke, took over the business in 1945 and constructed the Pathoekeweg building. With his children he founded the Chocolaterie Kathy in 1979. Since

1984 its products have been sold in the Netherlands, France, Germany and Great Britain. In 1986 it extended its production throughout the world and, naturally, it needed to expand further: a 9,600 square metre factory was built at Kolvestraat. Today, with its 145-strong labour-force, Kathy exports 70 per cent of its products, with a turnover of one billion Belgian francs.

(*Kathy Chocolaterie,
84, Pathoekeweg, 8000 Brugge.
Tel.: 050/32.06.92.
Fax: 050/32.02.01*).

## • Meurisse

In 1845 the young and dynamic Adolphe Meurisse, originally from Mons but settled in Antwerp, began to make chocolate. This was the first Belgian chocolate works. He succeeded because of his use of exotic ingredients, with the precious cargoes being unloaded in the city's port, the Antwerp sugar refineries and above all because of professional craft skills. He installed a 12 horse-power drive machine, adding successively all the new items of equipment which would improve the chocolate making.

### A few dates:

1890: Meurisse's two sons, René and Albert, take over the management
1915: Jacques Meurisse, Albert's son, becomes chairman
1969: the firm amalgamates with General Biscuit to form General Chocolate. The factory goes on to employ nearly 800 people, and produce up to 10,000 tonnes each year
1986: General Chocolate is bought by Jacobs Suchard

### Specialities:

Today, Meurisse is the second brand in Belgium, with more than 15 per cent of the market in bars and batons. In the consumer's opinion, Meurisse chocolate is made with heart, sympathy and pleasure, traditionally and with widely appreciated ingredients.
Filled 200 g chocolate bars (banana, raspberry, etc.), small 50-g bars (milk, praline, hazelnuts, etc.), 55-g bâtons (whole hazelnuts in milk or white chocolate), 500-g dessert blocks for ice-creams and desserts, 75-g Big Nuts (toasted whole hazelnuts), and the famous 50-g "Zero" (milk and fondant version), which offers the contrast of a filling of chilled cocoa and a chocolate coating.
(*Meurisse Kraft Jacobs Suchard,
450, Brusselsesteenweg, 1500 Halle.
Tel: 02/362.31.11.
Fax: 02/362.38.40*).

## • Neuhaus

The Swiss Jean Neuhaus opened a pharmaceutical confectionery shop, with his pharmacist brother-in-law, in the Galerie de la Reine in Brussels in 1857. On the death of his brother-in-law, Jean Neuhaus turned to his son Frédéric, in Neuchâtel, who came to Brussels to study the craft of master confectioner. In due course he gradually replaced medicaments with sweets and chocolates. The Neuhaus business settled in Nos. 25-27, Galerie de la Reine, from 1857 onwards, and in surroundings unchanged since 1912 offers chocolates, pralines and Neuhaus confectionery. It is undoubtedly the only shop of this kind in continuous business since 1857. The shop presents all on its own the whole history of praline, which was invented here.

### A few dates:

1857: establishment of the Neuhaus firm
1895: on the death of Frédéric, Jean Neuhaus (grandson of the founder) takes over the business under the name of Chocolaterie Neuhaus-Perrin

### Belgium, the land of welcome

A number of chocolate manufacturers have set up business in Belgium, such as Ferrero Ardennes. One of these, the Nestlé (Belgilux) company, has been here for a long time. It was in 1867 that Henri Nestlé invented his milk powder, in Vevey (Switzerland). He sold the business in 1875, and in 1905 it merged with the Anglo-Swiss Condensed Milk Company.

The first sale of chocolate under the 'Nestlé' brand name was in 1904. By 1925 the Belgian and French markets were separate, with the Nestlé company preparing to run its own production. Following its merger with Peter, Cailler, Kohler and Chocolats Suisses, Nestlé expanded from 1929 onwards to six chocolate factories in Turkey, France, Italy, Great Britain, Germany and Belgium. In 1932, local manufacturing increased. In Belgium this took the form of a milk factory in Hamoir. Between 1947 and 1990 the history of the company was marked by mergers, acquisitions and association with other companies - from Maggy, Crosse & Blackwell, Findus, Vittel and L'Oréal, to Buitoni-Perugina and Rowntree, more closely identified with chocolate.

In 1988 Nestlé bought Rowntree, and thereafter chocolate bars such as Kitkat, Nuts or Lion, filled milk chocolate beans such as Smarties and the small soft Yes cakes became part of its worldwide production.

Today, Nestlé has more than 400 production centres across five continents. The success of its products is undeniable: After Eight, Quality Street, Galak and Crunch are all part of its range.

• Nestlé Belgilux
221 rue de Birmingham,
1070 Brussels.
Tel.: 02/529.52.52
Fax: 02/529.56.00

*Wrapping for the famous*
*"After Eight" chocolate mints from Nestlé*

1912: creation of praline
1915: creation of the ballotin (carton) for pralines by Jean Neuhaus and his wife, Louise Agostini. The latter, an artist, goes on to create the "green and gold" colours and the "N" which are still used today
1918: Visit of the Prince of Wales and the young Prince Léopold, the future king

In March 1997 the chocolate makers Neuhaus first appeared on the Brussels stock exchange, in the spot market (double fixing). The Artal international group offered 60 per cent of its capital for sale, 450,000 shares, at a price between 1600 and 1,750 Belgian francs. 150,000 shares were offered to small investors.

According to stock exchange analysts, Neuhaus shares are the only representatives of their sector in Brussels. Sales are increasing annually by 10 per cent, the cash-flow by 13 per cent, the results of the operation by more than 20 per cent. Up to the year 2001, the dividend should grow by 14 per cent, and by 5 per cent thereafter.

Neuhaus is focussing on development in the home market, but also on growth in its activities in other countries- it exports its products to 36 different countries ! The challenge for Neuhaus is to become better known (for example in France with "Jeff de Bruges"). The stock exchange quotation was therefore also a fine marketing operation.

1924: Jean Neuhaus's son-in-law, Adelson De Gavre, runs the business. He goes on to share this responsibility with his son Pierre. Creation of two specialities: "Caprice" and "Tentation"

1969: Neuhaus is taken over by the Ceuppens group

1970: the factory moves to Zellik

1978: the chocolate-makers Jean-Jacques and Claude Poncelet, also managers of the Verhaeren and Mondose companies (soon to be joined by Corné Port Royal) take over management of the business

1987: 130th anniversary. Takeover by the Tirlemont Refinery

1989: Transfer to the new factory at Vlezenbeek

Neuhaus becomes the majority holder in the Paris company created by Philippe Jambon, "Jeff de Bruges"

1995: Neuhaus buys the Union Edel Chocolade in Haarlem, the Dutch "chocolate city"

Neuhaus enters a joint venture to distribute Neuhaus pralines in Japan

Neuhaus also acquires 55 per cent of the capital of the company responsible for distributing Neuhaus pralines in the U.S.A.

*The Neuhaus shop in the Galerie de la Reine, Brussels.*

1997: Neuhaus buys Martial, the company which specialises in distributing chocolates and sugar confectionery in France. The Neuhaus-Mondose group covers the Neuhaus, Mondose, Jeff de Bruges, Union Edel Chocolade and Martial brands and is part of the Artal group, an international holding company diversifying into the food industry

1997 is a significant year for Neuhaus, with the introduction of its shares onto the Brussels stock exchange

## Specialities:

"Caprice" and "Tentation" pralines: a mixture of hazelnuts, almonds and caramelised sugar in a nougatine, shaped into a triangle and coated in dark chocolate in the case of "Caprice" and milk chocolate for "Tentation". The concern for detail is worth noting: instead of being white, as usual, the paper container - printed with an "N" - which holds the praline is of the same pale yellow as the carton itself. Neuhaus produces 2,000 tonnes per year and the company exports to 36 different countries. Neuhaus is on sale in 52 shops in Belgium (of which a dozen are owned by the company, "... for it is a matter of personal knowledge of the business of retail sales, to understand the customer", explains Philippe Van Coppenolle, marketing director), and from more than 100 sales points in pâtisseries. Neuhaus is distributed to 400 shops in Germany, 200 in the United States, 72 in Japan (via Nihon Neuhaus).
(Neuhaus, 2, Postweg,
1602 Vlezembeek.
Tel: 02/568.22.11.
Fax: 02/568.22.07).

## Sky Shops: the world's biggest sales point

With 500 tons of chocolate sold each year, the Sky Shops at Zaventem airport (Brussels National Airport) are the largest sellers of chocolate in the world. Whether they are in the old terminal (Self Service, Kiosque Neuhaus), in the satellite (Self Service), in the new terminal (Kiosque Neuhaus, Godiva, duty and tax free), or in the two Last Minute Shops, it must be recognised, with pleasure, that Belgian chocolate (Godiva, Daskalidès, Corné Port-Royal, Mondose, Wittamer, Guylian, Côte d'Or and Galler) is keenly sought by French, Belgian, British, German or Spanish passengers.

In terms of quantity, Asian customers are far ahead as consumer-travellers. The kiosks where pralines can be selected individually appear to be the most successful. There are regular special promotions: the presence of a chocolate maker who comes to enrobe his manons on the spot, cartons of Easter eggs given away free ... all add to the attractions of these display windows of the European capital city, open to the whole world !

*"October is the best month, followed by December", says M. Marc Leemans, the commercial director of Belgian Sky Shops Ltd. Our sales are undoubtedly lower in summer. The "charter" passenger does not buy pralines, if he is on his way to one of the "costas", for example. But July sales still reach 66 per cent of December sales, which is far above the levels for shops in town. Our sales prices are the same as in the shops ... less the VAT."*

### Location of six sales points:

Kiosque Neuhaus: Neuhaus products are on sale, not pre-packed, in the old terminal.
Self Service: all the brands are on sale, self-service, in the old terminal.
Satellite: all the brands are on self-service sale in the Satellite.
Kiosque Neuhaus and Godiva: these two brands are on sale, loose, in the new terminal.
Duty & Tax Free: self-service for all brands in the new terminal.
Last Minute Shops: two shops located near Gates B offer mainly Neuhaus and Godiva goods.

• S.A. Belgian Sky Shops,
Brussels National Airport,
1930 Zaventem.
Tel.: 02/715.10.20.
Fax: 02/721.39.96.

# Some chocolate novelties

## • Charlemagne's Farm

Appreciated as far away as the Court of Japan, Charlemagne's Farm lies at the very heart of the Carolingian dynasty, for this is where Charlemagne himself was born. In order to respect the building constructed in the 17th century (with its foundations dating from the year 1000 !), the entire modern factory lies within the old walls. During the 1980s Madame Denise Courant-Bellefroid - following her hotel-trade training in Liège and specialist study of the history of cooking, particularly in the Middle Ages and the Renaissance - evolved a completely new concept to bring chocolate to the peak of originality: a dark chocolate with its flavour in the block. This was a new development: hitherto, the flavour lay in the the filling inside the chocolate coating.

After various trials with chocolate flavoured with spices or Turkish coffee, she launched out seven years ago, with great boldness, into the production of flower-flavoured chocolate. In a different direction, she responded to her customer's requests and extended her range of products. This in turn led to the creation of a line of truffles which met with great success, thanks to a craftsman style of presentation and a specific recipe: natural, dietetic and gourmet, resulting in a light truffle with a minimal amount of sugar. And there are truffles made of plain super-quality chocolate, with brandy, calvados, orange, hazelnuts, or Oriental coffee. Sales of these truffles, and also of the finest pralines, is reserved exclusively for luxury specialist shops (in particular "Le Pain quotidien"), the great five star hotels and first class services (British Airways).

Aimed at exports, the house of Charlemagne sells 95 per cent of its production to foreign markets: Sweden, Saudi Arabia, France, Japan, the United States, Great Britain, Germany, etc.

Charlemagne chocolate is frequently honoured. When Prince Philippe visited Istanbul he was given a supply of "Topsy Turvy"; this collection contains an unexpected assortment of chocolates with spices, coffee, tea, citrus fruits, classic fruits, and flowers, the jewel of the "Topsy Turvy" range.

*(Chocolaterie Charlemagne, 8, place Jacques-Brel, 4400 Herstal. Tel.: 04/264.66.44).*

## • Café-Tasse

**The meeting of two universal flavours**

After working with Neuhaus and Godiva, François Decarpentrie decided in 1988 to create a range of chocolates to eat over coffee, at home or in a restaurant. Thus were born the "Napolitains" from Café-Tasse: small, square, unfilled chocolates.

The packaging is made of natural products, uniquely composed of recycled materials: kraft paper, wood, jute, etc. Success came immediately, and the range was very quickly extended to offer other specialities: "Santos", for example, grains of coffee coated with chocolate. The concern for detail extends to offering a dark decaffeinated Santos ! Today, the company offers its Chocolates News (with the first issue appearing in July 1996), and has set up its own Internet site, proof of its dynamic attitue. It is a matter of maintaining contact with the 25 countries where its products are sold: France, where after a year, the company already has 600 sales points, with Galeries Lafayette, or Spain with El Corte Inglès, as well as Australia with Myers Store, the United States with Saks Fifth Avenue, or Singapore, Taiwan, Korea, Hong Kong, etc.

"Why should a sector as traditional and conservative as chocolate send you a News?" wrote François Decarpentrie. "Because we would like to be closer to our customers, who are our partners. We would also like to encourage others to share our enthusiasm ..."

There has been a "Café-Tasse Store" in the Grand-Place in Brussels since September 1994. Ceramic coffee and chocolate services can also be bought there.

Originally, the cups were designed for internal staff use. The demands of customers were so pressing that the collection, hand-made by Belgian craftsmen, is now on sale in the shop for everyone to buy !
(Café-Tasse, 57, Chaussée de Tubize, 1440 Wauthier-Braine.
Tel: 02/366.96.14.
Fax: 02/366.90.32).

### • *Dolfin*
**Imagination and creativity !**
The passion for chocolate may be inherited, since Michaël and Jean-François Poncelet, the founders of Dolfin, are the sons of Jean-Jacques Poncelet - for several years director, with his brother Claude, of the chocolate makers Verhaeren, Mondose, Corné Port-Royal and Neuhaus !

Michaël declares: "We have always heard chocolate spoken of with love, and we retain the memory of those craftsmen whose movements, repeated a thousand-fold but never carelessly, symbolised the pride of creating these marvellous mouthfuls".

Created in 1989, the Dolfin company originally produced personalised napolitains, the little chocolate squares designed to be served with coffee in restaurants, hotels, etc. In 1996, Dolfin created its own brand, and added to the napolitains a 70 g bar, of which the shape offered free rein to the creative imagination. This took Dolfin out of the Belgian tradition because the chocolate was not filled, but the ingredients, entirely natural, were incorporated directly into it. This distinctive technique respects the purity and strength of flavours and blends them harmoniously. It also offers the advantage that it keeps better.

The range of bars which evolved out of the Poncelet brothers' researches is currently available in 14 different flavours: from dark chocolate with preserved orange peel to mint leaves, pink pepper, etc. Chocolate squares, weighing 5 g, are available in 13 flavours: dark Earl Grey, cinnamon milk, 88 per cent dark chocolate, etc. The managers of this medium-sized company won the First Prize for Imagination and Creativity at SIAL, the great Paris food fair. *(Dolfin SA, 59, chaussée de Tubize, 1440 Wauthier-Braine.*
*Tel.: 02/366.24.24.*
*Fax: 02/366.22.42).*

## • *"Italo-Suisse"*
### Chocolate Figures
One of the most highly specialised Belgian firms, which makes chocolate figurines, is called "Italo-Suisse" ! The origins of this name date back to the travels, for study and final training in chocolate, of the founder, Joseph Libert, in France, Italy and Switzerland ...

In 1924 he set up the Belgian "Italo-Suisse" company in Izegem and later moved to Roulers. In 1951 Antoine Libeert and his wife took over the management and continued to expand the company until it finally settled in Comines in 1975 and specialised in hollow chocolate figures. This specialisation was taken over by the four children of the family in 1985: Myriam, Pieter, Luc and Ignace. The two heaviest periods of their production are naturally at Easter (chocolate eggs) and in December (St Nicolas and Christmas). In 1991 His Highness Prince Albert opened a new division, producing bars and batons made of milk, dark and white chocolate and with hazelnuts.

This range was then extended with the manufacture of filled bars, and completed with a range of pralines or chocolate flavoured with praline, coffee, caramel, nougat, and other exquisite aromas.

(Italo-Suisse, 107A avenue des Châteaux, 7780 Comines. Tel: 056/56.05.05)

## • *Planète Chocolat*
On 6 December 1995 (St Nicolas's Day), Frank Duval opened "Planète Chocolat" close to the Grand-Place in Brussels. His

# ITALO-SUISSE

concept was the creation of food as art. He made contact with artists who designed new praline shapes for him. After a year of research, he developed a new technique for making moulds, a mixture of sculpture and engraving. Artists such as Eric Leloup, Jean-Christophe Alix and Martin Szkely created original designs for him.

Frank Duval is the owner of the Duval chocolate factory, where the main activity is manufactu-ring to order for establishments looking for personalised gifts. A craft-based company, it produces only 5-10 tonnes per year. Frank Duval also owns Planète Chocolat. The first feature of this shop-studio-museum lies in making chocolate in the display window ! Upstairs is a refreshment room and an exhibition gallery. "This place reflects my vision of chocolate. Here you will find only products that I like: you can, for example, enjoy a hot chocolate with a croissant in a calm but modern ambience," explains Frank Duval. This intimate area, decorated in red and gold, also sells vegetable quiches, wine and tea.

This enthusiast came to chocolate through Christian Nihoul, where he was employed in the catering service, and through an RTBF programme devoted to food art, which inspired his own project.

*(Planète Chocolat, 57, rue du Midi, 1000 Brussels.*
*Tel.: 02/511.07.55).*

# Chocolate bars

Total exports of chocolate amount to 212,465 tonnes, worth more than 30 billion Belgian francs.

Coating chocolate represents 41 per cent of these exports, batons and bars 20 per cent, and pralines nearly 10 per cent.

The economic and financial statistical service of the Belgian National Bank recognises three categories of bars and batons:

1. Filled chocolates: 14 per cent (870 million Belgian francs).
As with all categories, France is the leading destination for Belgian exports (36 pert cent), followed by the Netherlands (30 per cent), Austria (9 per cent), and the United Kingdom (5 per cent).

2. Chocolates with cereals, nuts or fruit: 37 per cent (1,870 million Belgian francs).
France beats all records in this category (54 per cent), followed this time by Germany (18 per cent) and Russia (17 per cent).

3. Unfilled chocolates: 49 per cent (2.5 billion Belgian francs).
France continues to lead the field (46 per cent), followed by the Netherlands (21 per cent), Germany (17 per cent) and Russia (7 per cent). On 4 April 1928 Coenraad Johannes Van Houten registered his patent for "powdered chocolate", created in a press which extracted the cocoa butter, chocolate appeared in solid form.

At first it was sold in bars, and also in the form of figurines and chocolate drops (known in Belgium as "caraques", because of the use of Caracas cacao). In Amsterdam in 1840, Bensdorp made bars which were individually wrapped instead of being sold loose, as hitherto. Among the anecdotes which stand out in the history of the chocolate bar, there was the creation of a bar ordered by her Queen Victoria with her effigy on

it (we may be permitted to refer in passing to a brand of chocolate with the same name !). The queen sent the bars to her troops engaged in the Boer War in South Africa, to wish them a happy new year in 1900. We should also mention the appearance in 1911 of

the famous gold and white paper wrapping used for Côte d'Or chocolate bars.

In 1913 the Swiss Jules Séchaud launched the first filled bar. Until 1920, bars weighed between 150 and 1000 grammes.

In the 1930s the price of a 400-g bar of milk chocolate ranged from 5.90 Belgian francs (Van Loo) to 10 BF (Meyers).

## *Batons*

The name "baton" is a Belgian expression - elsewhere the usual term is simply a chocolate bar. The chocolate baton is a Belgian invention: Kwatta's launch in 1921 of these small chocolate bars, weighing between 30 and 45 grammes, was very quickly copied by all the other chocolate manufacturers in Belgium.

At the 1935 Exhibition, Côte d'Or displayed an "entirely automatic" machine: one side contained liquid chocolate, while on the other a continuous belt delivered the chilled batons.
In 1936, Jacques launched a baton

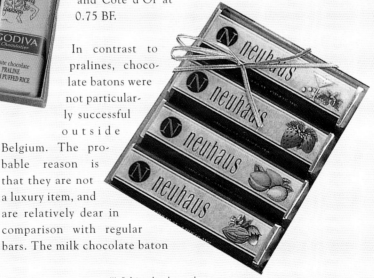

filled with praline. At the time, batons cost one franc each, but Victoria sold them at 0.90 BF and Côte d'Or at 0.75 BF.

In contrast to pralines, chocolate batons were not particularly successful outside Belgium. The probable reason is that they are not a luxury item, and are relatively dear in comparison with regular bars. The milk chocolate baton

with all kinds of filling was and remains a typically Belgian product. 9,700 tonnes of batons are produced each year, representing 12 per cent of the world market.

# Spreads

This is another invention in which Belgians can take pride: it was in Belgium that the spreading paste was invented. There was "Choco-pasta" and "Pastador" (created by Côte d'Or in 1960 and relaunched in 1980) and "Kwatta"; the custom for children to cover their bread at breakfast time with a special spreading paste is a recent development. The Belgians have become the greatest consumers of this item, accounting for between 800 g and 1 kg per year each. 90 per cent of spreads are flavoured with hazelnuts, and two companies dominate the market: Ferrero and All Crump.

| | |
|---|---|
| Nutella (Ferrero) | 60 % |
| Crumpasta, Tartinut (All Crump) | 30 % |
| Kwatta (Continental Foods) | 23 % |

Imports of this product match exports almost exactly; however, Belgium imports 2,700 t from Italy and 1,600 t from France, while exports go mainly to France (4,500 t).

The market for hazelnut chocolate alone represents a total of 1.4 billion Belgian francs.

| | |
|---|---|
| Wallonia | 833 g per head |
| Flanders | 715 g per head |
| Brussels | 541 g per head |

Statistically, consumption is greater in more modest households with larger families. Chocolate spread represents 0.6 per cent of the average Belgian household expenditure, while coffee represents 4 per cent.

# Chocolate biscuits

The origins of the biscuit ("twice baked") lie in its supreme convenience as a form of food for soldiers and sailors. It was only in the 19th century that the English began to bake a more delicate version of this basic item of grocery: the sweet biscuit. They are no longer designed to check hunger, but are a delicacy to serve with tea. Huntley's were responsible for the modern sweet biscuit, with the invention in 1830 of the biscuit machine. This is a type of biscuit casting machine, in which they are shaped before being baked.

In Belgium, Edward De Beukelaere left his rural background to settle in Antwerp in 1855, where he made the first sweet biscuits in an ordinary kitchen oven and displayed these delicacies with the bread and cakes in his pâtisserie. He built his first factory in 1870.

Other pioneers also took an interest in biscuits: Jechers, Bossaert and Carlier founded the Victoria biscuit factory in 1896, a title which evoked the Queen of England and the fame of English biscuits. In 1890 Edouard Parein, a cereal grower, bought Joseph Cordeman's biscuit factory in Borgerhout for his son. Despite the harmony between De Beukelaere and Parein, it was not until 1965 that the two businesses joined forces and became the General Biscuit Company, which soon afterwards bought Guglielmone Biscotti (Italy), Victoria and L'Alsacienne. In 1977 the company became part of the Ceraliment-LU-Brun group and was renamed the General Biscuit Belgïe.

Chocolate appears twice in the preparation of biscuits - either in the filling, when chocolate powder is added to the basic ingredients of sugar and fats, or as coating, when the three most frequently used chocolates are fondant or milk chocolate, or the intermediate "half-and-half" type. The operation of adding the chocolate coating is done with special machines which cover the biscuits completely or partially by dipping them into a container of heated chocolate. To achieve its typical shine and hardness, the liquid chocolate should be tempered on the biscuits: it is chilled from 45 degrees Centigrade to 28-29 degrees in several meticulously timed stages.

A survey undertaken by Marketing Unit places biscuit consumers in the "acceptance/personality" sector, the same as for chocolate, with the added element of greater impulsiveness where chocolate is concerned. In 1995 Belgian confectionery production exceeded 560,000 tonnes for all sweetened confectionery combined (chocolates, biscuits, sweets), of which 45 per cent were consumed within the Belgian market. There are no fewer than 100,000 confectionery sales points in Belgium; Chobisco, the royal syndical chamber, is a non-profit-making organisation designed to serve the whole confectionery industry. Twenty thousand people are employed, with about 500 craftsmen and small, medium and large companies.

# Confectionery bars

Confectionery bars are by far the most widely sold products in Belgium. They represent 30 per cent of the overall total, with 24,000 tonnes per year. The characteristic of this snack item is that chocolate is not - as with the filled baton - the primary ingredient. As this is a less expensive product it is naturally eaten mostly by young people; it has been observed that 91.2 per cent of Belgian households with children buy snack chocolate items. Those who eat bars and batons are looking for real chocolate, while confectionery bars differ in forming mini-meals to satisfy hunger. They are seen as supplying more energy and enjoy a more modern or fashionable image. This is no doubt why 92 per cent of sales take place in large self-service stores.

We owe the invention of the confectionery bar to an American, Milton Snavely Hershey, who in 1900 invented "Hershey's Kisses", the most widely sold commercial sweets in the United States: the factory produces 33 million per day ! But the great fashion for these bars dates more precisely from 1923, when Mars launched the "Milky Way".

In 1932 his son Forrest Mars launched the "Mars" with milk and caramel (two million units per day) and the famous slogan, "A Mars a day !" In the 1930s other companies throughout the world followed the fashion. In the Netherlands, Nuts invented his hazelnut bar with malt extract, and in England Rowntree launched "Kit-Kat" (1935), "Rolo" (1937) and "Smarties" (1937), of which 10 billion tubes are produced each year in Britain. At the end of the 1970s the same company invented the "Lion" bar. (Rowntree was bought by Nestlé in 1988, which added its own confectionery bar, the "Yes"). In Belgium, De Beukelaer very soon came up with the famous "Zip".

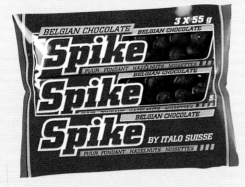

# Chocolate drinks

There are two types of drink based on cocoa, or chocolate flavoured drinks: instant powder to be mixed with milk, and cocoa in ready-to-drink liquid form. Belgians consume 60 million litres each year ! Of this total, the instant product represents 70 per cent and the liquid, 30 per cent.

The growth of this sector is estimated at 3-5 per cent per year. European consumption is as follows:

1. Spain            1,250 g per head
2. Switzerland    1,045 g per head
3. France            948 g per head
4. Germany         765 g per head
5. Belgium          370 g per head
6. Great Britain   364 g per head
7. Italy              110 g per head
8. The Netherlands 105 g per head

These differences cannot be explained either by differences between northern and southern countries, or by climatic influences. The variations probably have historic origins. In any case, it can be seen that the potential for expansion in this market is considerable.

Instant chocolate is consumed above all (60 per cent) by children under 12 years of age, while liquid chocolate drinks are mostly favoured by consumers between 15 and 24 years. In both cases, it is the mother of the

family who buys it. For those under 12, the motive is above all to encourage children to drink milk, milk containing the calcium and phosphorus which are so important to growth. 47 per cent of them drink it at breakfast-time.

## From Kwatta to Nesquik

In the beginning it was the Kwatta brand which dominated the Belgian market; but the powder was reluctant to dissolve, making it unsuitable for mixing with milk, and so it was destined for adult consumption.

In the 1950s Nesquik gradually redirected the product towards the younger consumer. Because it mixes instantly, it is suitable for drinking hot or cold.

### Instant Drinking Chocolate:
Nesquik (Nestlé)            50 %
Ovomaltine (Wander)          7 %
Kwatta (Continental Foods)  3 %

### Liquid Drinking Chocolate:
Cécémel (Nutricia)          29 %
Liquid Nesquik (Nestlé)      5 %

We should not forget that most dairy companies also offer a chocolate-flavoured milk, in particular Stabilac (the milk industry's second most popular brand, with 13 per cent of the market).

*Crushing cocoa beans
(Godiva).*

# IV. The guide to Belgian praline manufacturers

A detailed selection of fifty praline
manufacturers: their background,
shops and products
(Rate of currency exchange:
60 Belgian Francs/£1)

# Arosa

*La Maison du chocolat artisanal*
*67, rue Marché-aux-Herbes, 1000 Brussels.*
*Tel.: 02/513.78.92.*
*(Open: 10.00-19.00 h, closed Sunday*
*and Monday morning).*

## Background

Arosa has been in existence for more than 30 years (28, Helst, 2630 Aartselaar. Tel: 03/877.35.30), and at the shop in the Rue Marché-aux-Herbes for about ten years. Madame Eva Van Peborgh and her son have been independent from the factory for the last six years but retain a sales agreement: three-quarters of their products are made at Aartselaar.

## The Shop

The shop in the heart of tourist Brussels is fresh and clean. The assistant uses an enormous plastic glove to make up the cartons, which are rather attractive in themselves.

## The Products

The shop offers 52 different pralines. Note the vanilla and coffee manons, and the assortments of truffles and bitter chocolates. Price: 790 BF/kg.

# L'Art de Praslin

*12, rue de Nivelles, 1300 Wavre.*
*Tel.: 010/22.32.40.*
*(Open: Monday-Saturday, 9.00-12.30 h*
*and 13.30-18.30 h).*
*(Shops in Wavre, Namur and Brussels).*

*"We did not launch out into chocolate, we were born to it." Joël Stevens*

## Background

This family business was founded in Brussels in 1938, and moved to Wavre in 1958. Its production is entirely hand-made. There is no machinery in the workshop, because the work is done with moulds and base and built up with a spoon or case. Madame Edwige Stevens, the manager, is helped by Joël Stevens, five craftsmen and three assistants.

## The Shop

The visit was to the Brussels shop (59, avenue du Roi-Chevalier, 1200 Brussels). The prices are clearly marked. White paper is used for wrapping, gathered with a ribbon and a flower.

## The Products

130 varieties of praline. Specially created praline can also be ordered. The well-known specialities are the manons, iced truffles (praline whipped with fresh cream, shaped with a spoon and candied) and cerisettes, made with cherries. For lovers of manons, this is the only establishment to offer

three kinds: white, coffee and chocolate fondant. The little liqueur bonbons with crisp coating and the orangettes are excellent. There are several cups which are filled and sealed with chocolate, by hand, which is unusual. Price: 1,080 BF/kg.

# Bertrand

*30 rue des Croisiers, 5000 Namur.*
*Tel.: 081/22.34.35. (Open: daily, 9.00-18.00h).*

*"A chocolate-maker's life enables the use of the imagination..." "My regret: not to have a second life, to give me time to show my pralines to Americans because they love them so much !" M. Bertrand*

### Background

André Bertrand has been established in the heart of Namur since 1960. This is a family business: his son Max works with him since he too underwent a very distinguished training as a chocolate maker, crowned with great distinction.

### The Shop

The shop is sober and modern, designed to display the chocolate to advantage. Air conditioning operates through to the workshop, which is on the first floor and includes a laboratory for coating and moulding. André Bertrand is an enthusiastic and whole-hearted craftsman ; for example, he buys hazelnuts in Piedmont, and Turkish pistachios which he grinds himself. Madame Bertrand uses pretty little gloves to pick out the pralines. The carton is

IV. The guide to Belgian praline manufacturers

Belgian chocolate

bordeaux red with a gilded design of Namur fort. The prices are shown, and even translated into French francs for the many tourists who cross the frontier.

## The Products

The chocolatier Bertrand makes more than 50 different pralines. New varieties of both shape and flavour are constantly being introduced, according to season and current trends. The freshness of the product is the key concept in their preparation. Some specialities: "Délices de Namur", consisting of two different praline creams, one with a light addition of alcohol, the other dark and more baked, and "Thé indien", ("Indian Tea"). The ganaches are always light. Among other specialities, we should note the particularly succulent almond creams, and a preference for the ginger and orange flavours. Price: 550 BF/kg.

# The Chocolate Line

*19, rue Simon-Stevinplein, 8000 Bruges.*
*Tel.: 050/34.10.90.*
*(Open: daily, 10.00-19.00 h. Closed Monday and Thursday, 13.00-14.00 h).*

*"Chocolate is a raw material which offers enormous scope for flavour, to which is added the charm of unusual presentation. All this inspires us to create and to invent. Making chocolate is therefore a craft profession which offers tremendous personal satisfaction." Dominique and Fabienne Persoone*

## Background

The shop and workshop-annex were opened in July 1992. As with most small businesses, it is run by a married couple, Dominique and Fabienne Persoone-De Staercke. Dominique attended the hotel school "De Groene Poorte" in Bruges and spent a year in Paris at the Pavillon Montsouris, where the kitchens are directed by Jean-Michel Bouvier, formerly with Michel Guérard and Senderens. On his return he was taken on at the starred restaurant Le Bouquet, at the Middelkerke casino, where he took charge of the pâtisserie. He returned to France for some further advanced training courses, and benefited on this occasion from the experience of Pierre Hermes and Pascal Brustein, two of the best practitioners in France. Fabienne, meanwhile, had an artistic training and looks after sales and presentation. A sales assistant, Angie, provides efficient support and the family all joins in to help at weekends.

## The Shop

The shop is light, clean, tidy and handsome. A large window divides the shop from the workshop. On one side of the shop a counter holds the pralines on square dishes. Glass containers display truffles, mousses, block chocolate, etc. On the other side, a table presents the "delights of the month" in chocolate, such as Chinese figures, animals, houses. Another table has marzipans, preserves and cakes made on the premises. The welcome is friendly, the carton is very attractive.

IV. The guide to Belgian praline manufacturers

## The Products

Everything is made on the spot, under the customer's eye, and therefore has to be supremely fresh. The Chocolate Line has added some exotic flavours to the classic range, such as tea and mint pralines. There are moulded pralines, and coated ones. There is a great variety of fillings, and truffles made with butter and fresh cream, as well as an excellent almond paste. The white truffle with coconut is delicious. There are also little biscuits, with a foundation of flaky pastry with honey and chocolate, madeleines and jam squares on a base of home-made flaky pastry. The pralines are priced at 1,000 BF/kg.

# Patrick Claude

*Hand-made Chocolates, 1, rue de la Justice, 5100 Wépion. Tel.: 081/46.28.64.*
*Sales outlets: Le Comptoir de l'Oliviat (89, rue de la Croix, 5000 Namur. Tel.: 081/23.14.98), Diffalux (55, Rue de Jausse, 5100 Nannine. Tel.: 081/40.13.00). Pâtisserie Michel Lebutte (10954, chaussée de Dinant, 5100 Wépion. Tel.: 081/46.01.12), La Ferme Landaise (41, place Sainte-Catherine, 1000 Brussels. Tel.: 02/512.95.39), and Epicerie fine (510, chaussée de Bruxelles, 1410 Waterloo. Tel.: 02/354.55.44)*

*"The noble quality of a substance such as chocolate demands that for the manufacture of pralines, for example, products of the highest quality are used.*

*That is the only way to produce something good, and when it is good, there is nothing better."*
*Patrick Claude*

## Background

M. André Claude, after apprenticeship with the greatest Belgian chocolate and confectionery experts of the 1940s, set up his shop in the Charleroi area. In 1996 Patrick Claude decided to follow the family tradition of developing new creations that combine the classic with the modern. After a year of existence, there are numerous plans: periods with Gaston Lenôtre in Paris and at a school for the best craftsmen in France, at Yssingeaux.

## The Products

The chocolats are made with ingredients of the highest quality: fresh cream or spirits. The bitter chocolate used contains 70 per cent cocoa, and the flavour is achieved through mixtures blended on the premises. There is, for example, a dark chocolate truffle made to a recipe created in 1932, a bitter dark chocolate with oriental filling consisting of preserved ginger stem and hand-made marzipan, or the magnificent "pyramid" with bitter and white chocolate applied with a brush, filled with butter, white chocolate, an infusion of pure Arabica coffee, and Perigord walnut kernels !

The craftsman foresees the creation of new products: cinnamon pralines, fresh raspberry or marinated blackcurrant ganache, with bergamot, fruit and nut *mendiants* made with dried fruit and Malaga raisins macerated in Armagnac and passion fruit...

# Corné Port-Royal

*SA Vanparys, 10 avenue Mercator, ZI Wavre-Nord, 1300 Wavare. Tel.: 010/24.13.66. (Head Office: 50 Avenue Rogier, 1030 Brussels.) 40 sales outlets, including 13 in Brussels.*

## Background

Monsieur Corné founded his chocolate business in the 1930s. Disagreements divided the family into two companies: Corné Toison d'Or and Corné de France. The latter carried on production only in France and sold its Belgian interests to Neuhaus-Mondose. To avoid confusion, Corné became Corné Port-Royal in Belgium. In 1990 the Vanparys company (created by Englebert Vanparys in 1920) bought the brand. Today, Robert Vanparys is the chairman and André, his son, the managing director of this company with a 222-million Belgian franc turnover and annual production of 400 tonnes.

## The Shop

We visited the shop at 9 Rue de la Madeleine, 1000 Brussels. (Tel.: 02/512.43.14. Open: daily, 10.00-19.30h) The shop is clean and welcoming. The design is calm, with plenty of natural wood, to create a very appealing atmosphere of intimacy. The cartons are gilded and coloured.

## The Chocolates

There are 66 types of Corné-Port-Royal pralines. The oldest specialities are "Javanais" and "Ope-ra", and vanilla and coffee manons. Look for the iced truffle ("truffe glacé") and the golden disc ("palet d'or"). Price: 940 BF/kg.

# Corné toison d'or

*Godiva SA. 5, rue de l'Armistice, 1081 Brussels. Tel.: 02/422.17.11.*

## Background

Founded around 1930 by Monsieur Corné, the company divided into Corné Côte de France (see Corné Port-Royal) and Corné Toison d'Or. In 1989, Godiva bought Corné Toison d'Or from members of the Corné family.

## The Shop

This is at 23 Galerie du Cinquantenaire, 1040 Brussels (Tel.: 02/733.95.55) in one of the oldest shopping galleries in Brussels. In the shop, which extends in width, the counter lies along the window and offers little space to stand back and have a good look at the display. The old light fittings and painted panelling give an old-style atmosphere to the shop which is not without charm. The carton is made up with great care in front of the customer.

## The Products

The pralines are large, typical of Brussels style, and are hand-made. Corné Toison d'Or is famous for its "Mireille" (a manon with glossy sugar coating on a vanilla or coffee cream base). "Cendrillon" ("Cinderella"), under its coating of ganache made with fresh cream, reveals a blend of nougatine and mandarin cream. The choice is wide - some 80 hand-made chocolates - and well balanced. Price: 980 BF/kg.

# Crahay

*3, place des Carmes, 4000 Liège.*
*Tel.: 04/222.12.65.*
*102, rue Puits-en-Sock, 4000 Liège.*
*Tel.: 04/343.43.86*
*(Open Tuesday-Saturday, 10.00-18.30 h)*

*"We have created this whole business and everything that we sell is made in our workshops. We are following a craft and family tradition.." Michelle Crahay*

## Background

After a long period as confectioners and chocolate makers in Spa, Michelle and Ghislain Crahay settled in Liège to devote themselves to chocolate, first in Rue Puits-en-Sock and, eleven years later, Place des Carmes. This is a true family business, for their daughter is also involved in the manufacture.

## The Shop

The shop is clean, the welcome is smiling. The full range is on public display. The carton is classic: glossy white coated paper lined with gold, then wrapped in green or dark red paper. The prices are clearly marked and full details of the contents of the pralines are given.

## The Chocolates

The moulded pralines are in two colours. There are some very good ones made with fresh cream and an assortment of more than eight truffles (coffee nectar, champagne, armagnac soufflé, or the "Tchantès" truffle with gin...). An extensive additional range is based on almond paste. A distinctive item is a praline made with fresh cream with, inside, a filling of "sirop de Liège". Price: 960 BF/kg.

# Daskalidès

*1, Henegouwenstraat, 9000 Ghent.*
*Tel.: 09/224.36.77.*

## Background

Prodromos Daskalidès founded the business which bears his name in Ghent, and his wife went on to open other shops in Knokke, Liège and Brussels. In 1963 the refreshments room closed its doors. 1971 was the year when they bought the establishment in the Avenue Louise in Brussels. Jean and then Alexandre Daskalidès continued with the family business. The Ghent building, splendidly located behind the cathedral of Saint-Bavon, is a protected building. Daskalidès has a substantial distribution network.

## The Shop

This is at 277 Avenue Georges-Henry, 1200 Brussels (Woluwe-Saint-Lambert). (Open, Monday-Friday 9.00-13.00 and 14.00-19.00h, Saturday 9.00-19.00h. Tel.: 02/225.39.37.) The shop offers other products as well as pralines, it is air-conditioned, and the prices are listed. The cartons have a distinctive closure. The layers of pralines are divided by a paper which indicate that in 1987 the company received the "Golden Palm" for the quality and tradition of its chocolates.

## The Products

The speciality is indisputably the "coeur au citron", the "lemon heart".

# Debailleul

*406, Avenue Charles-Quint, 1083 Ganshoren.*
*Tel.: 02/469.05.35.*
*(Open: daily except Sunday and public holidays, 8.00-19.00 h; Saturdays, until 18.30 h)*

*"Our speciality? We aim at constant renewal, while remaining attentive to our clientele..." Marc Debailleul*

## Background

The Debailleul-Diffusion company has been in business since 1983, making fine patisserie, ice-creams and sorbets. In 1995 the full range of pralines was launched: it consists of moulded pralines (Belgian style), and coated pralines (French style). The chocolates are also on sale at Rob (Brussels) and certain caterers and sophisticated food retailers in Belgium, Berlin and Tokyo. They have recently been noted and awarded a prize by the French chocolate enthusiasts' society, the "Club des croqueurs de chocolat".

## The Shop

The shop is sober and stylish. Customers move round a central counter, made of bur walnut, to make their selection. The range of pralines in cartons is kept in a special refrigerator. They are available in two weights only, 250 g or 600 g. The carton is made of distinctive card which reproduces the shop's bur walnut style, and can contain 50 g, 125 g or 600 g of pralines.

## The Chocolates

The range of pralines includes milk and white chocolate and fondant (70 per cent cocoa solids). The filling is smooth, crisp, creamy or rich, depending on the ingredients. They vary from the classic - the range of different pralines - to the very sophisticated - ganaches flavoured with vanilla, fruit or tea - or the imaginative, such as a combination of ganache and fruit paste.

No colouring, preservative or additives are used in the preparation of the 100 per cent natural materials. All the pralines are deliberately small - approximately ten per 100 g, to increase the enjoyment of eating them. Price: 1,300 BF/kg.

DEBAILLEUL

Belgian chocolate

# Déesse

*Chocolaterie Déesse, sprl, 118, Wolterslaan, 9000 Ghent. Tel.: 09/228.15.27.*

*"Our aim is to offer a product which is entirely hand-made, and top of the range. This is how we aim to respond with enthusiasm and love of the craft to the greatest demands of our clientèle".*
*The De Sutter family*

## Background

The Déesse chocolate establishment was founded after the Second World War by Monsieur and Madame Josef De Sutter. Monsieur De Sutter undertook various training periods with the best confectioners in Ghent and began by selling his products in both French and Belgian Flanders. In 1975 the business became a limited company.
Josef's son Patrick gave a new thrust to the company and extended its clientele into northern France and Wallonia. Today Alexandre, the third generation of the De Sutter family, also works in the chocolaterie, having attended the hotel school "Ter Groene Poorte" in Bruges.

## The Shop

It should be noted that this praline manufacturer is a wholesaler (no retail sales); but it is sufficiently interesting not to be passed over in silence.

## The Products

The speciality is liqueur pralines using the major brands. Thus there is the "Marquise" (ganache, cognac, best brandy), or the "Merveilleux" (Grand-Marnier, chocolate cream), etc. The pralines are not too large, and the layer of chocolate is of substantial. There are plenty of moulded pralines. The finish is excellent.
Price: 1,000 BF/kg.

# De Hucorne-Fronville

*5, rue de Fer, 5000 Namur. Tel.081/22.23.72.*
*(Open: Monday-Saturday, 9.00-18.00 h).*
*(Also, since 1992: "La Maison des Desserts",*
*17, rue Haute-Marcelle, 5000 Namur.*
*Tel.: 081/22.74.51. Open: Tuesday-Sunday,*
*8.30-19.00 h)*

*"I practise this trade out of love of chocolate and... because I grew up in a craftsman's workshop."*
*Etienne de Hucorne*

## Background

The business was founded in 1946 by Madame Fronville and bought by her nephew Etienne de Hucorne in 1974, hence its double name.

## The Shop

The shop in the Rue de Fer is in the city's largest commercial artery, outside the pedestrianised area. The shop is small, narrow, decorated with porcelain ware. The atmosphere is classic. The pralines are placed delicately in the carton, to which ribbons are then added.

## The Products

The house specialities are the "Biétrumés de Namur": this is a soft butter and chocolate caramel, on a base of cooked fresh cream with toasted hazelnuts. The sugar manon is delicious. All the fresh-cream pralines are very good, and made from the finest quality ingredients. The flaky praline has a delicious after-taste of toasted dried fruit. Price: 990 BF/kg.

# Del Rey

5, Appelmansstraat, 2018 Antwerp.
Tel.: 03/233.29.37.
(Open: 9.00-18.30 h, except Sunday)

*"My father was a baker and I adore chocolate. In this trade, there are plenty of opportunities for experimenting with combinations of chocolate and various flavours..." Bernard Proot*

## Background

The business was founded in 1949. Today, it is the third generation, represented by Anne Seutin and Bernard Proot, which oversees its development and directs a team of 23 people ("Relais Dessert 1993")

## The Shop

This very fine shop is located in the heart of Antwerp, close to Le Meir. Its pastel décor is an effective combination of old and new. The large display counter holds 70 varieties of praline, on two or three shelves. The air-conditioning is pleasing, as is the welcome. There is a refreshment room next

to the shop. The sales girls, in spring colour uniforms, give well-informed advice with a smile. The prices are marked.

## The Products

The sugar manon is perfect, undoubtedly one of the best in Belgium. The orangettes are unusual and delicious. There is an excellent nougat with pistachio. The cherries with kirsch are unusual in style. Price: 1,350 BF/kg.

# Les Délices de Mélanie

27, rue Grétry, 1000 Brussels. Tel.: 02/217.90.31.
(Open: 10.30-18.30 h, Monday and Wednesday, to 19.30 on Thursday, Friday and Saturday).

*"In the constant search for quality and innovation we are looking for small-scale craftsmen who prepare their own products: liqueurs, fruit, etc. I test everything myself, and I am very demanding: this is the only way for a prestige shop to exist and stay in business, let alone prosper." Madame Nadine*

## Background

Mélanie Draps, a third-generation chocolate maker, decided to make truffles and then extended her range to include pralines. Madame Nadine's magnificent shop has been open since late 1994. Nothing had particularly predestined her for the chocolate business, but once in the profession not only did she learn all about it, undertake training and develop an interest in everything concerning chocolate, she became a true enthusiast. There are two more shops, in Stockel and Karreveld.

## The Shop

The shop is a model of its kind: crystal chandelier, light décor, in short everything which gives heart to a traditional chocolate shop. Madame Nadine serves with a smile (she admits to finding contact with customers very interesting, as if she were involved in psychotherapy...), using a glove, and she has an unbeatable knowledge of her products. She is also an expert in christenings, communions and weddings. The cartons are white and carry instructions on how to keep the contents fresh, and for how long. Nothing surprising, in this connection, to hear that Her Majesty the Queen of Belgium rings up from time to time to order a few things...

## The Products

Mélanie Draps offers 65 varieties of praline. She works with hand-made moulds. Her specialities include: 9 truffles, including "Mélanie" (a truffle coated with almonds), the "Rachmaninov" (a praline shaped like a musical instrument, made of pure ganache), almond paste, cherries in maraschino. The interest of the range is also that it is extensive enough to satisfy all tastes: it includes small pralines, and larger ones, sweeter and less sweet, genuine or "false" manons, etc. As the saying goes, "It is the customer who chooses and the customer who is right". Price: 950 BF/kg.

# Demaret

*89, voie de la Chocolaterie, 4651 Battice.*
*Tel.: 087/67.50.06.*
*(Open: in season, Monday-Thursday,*
*8.00-17.00 h and Friday, 8.00-12.30 h)*

*"Chocolate making is a trade directly descended from pâtisserie, which offers many opportunities for creating new flavours". Godefroid Demaret*

## Background

The business, founded in 1981, has four sales outlets in the region: Demaret Chocolatier, 90, rue de Heusy, 4800 Verviers; Pralinel, 22, rue Neuve, 4860 Pepinster; Pinnochio, 12 Klötzerbahn, 4700 Eupen; La Source des Manons, 58 rue Lamberts, 4840 Welkenraedt. Five members of the Demaret family are engaged in the business: Godefroid, Bethy, Nathalie, Corinne and Bénédicte.

## The Shop

We visited the shop in the Rue de Heusy, in Verviers. A wonderful curved display window houses a superb mounted text on chocolate: "Devilish temptation and divine comfort. Source of joy surrounded in mystery...". The shop is designed entirely in light wood, with jars and Limoges porcelain on the shelves; the walls have reproductions of old Verviers chocolate packaging: Defrance or Aiglon. The prices are clearly displayed. The packets are dazzling white and copper-coloured, and printed with the logo. On all sides the accent is on "the flavours of a great chocolate".

## The Products

This company makes more than 80 kinds of praline. Its specialities are the coated pralines, fresh cream manons, truffles, orangettes and mendiants. A special fruit manon is also promised. There is a range of dietary chocolate which contains no sugar.

# La Désirade

3, rue Chapell-Rahier, 4280 Lens-Saint-Remy (Hannut). Tel.: 019/51.08.07.

(Open: daily, except Thursday, 9.00-12.00 h and 13.30-18.30 h) (The parent house is at 73, rue Albert I$^{er}$. Tel.: 019/51.18.33. Open: 9.00-12.00 and 13.30-18.30 h, except Tuesdays).

"Chocolate is a passion in which I can express myself in many ways. I wanted to take up the challenge of working on the quality of fresh products, without added flavour or colouring, rather than quantity."
Dominique Docquier

## Background

The business was founded by the present-day director and maker, Dominique Docquier, and his wife, in July 1992. Monsieur Docquier has the diploma of the CERIA school and has worked with Nihoul, Schevenels and Galler.

## The Shop

The design is simple and the greeting friendly. Dominique Docquier himself sometimes comes in to the shop from the workshop behind, where he exercises his craft, to greet his customers. He makes up the selected carton with his gloved right hand. The packet resembles a jewel case.

## The Products

The house specialities are praline with péquet, white cinnamon log, cherry in maraschino, and fresh cream pralines. There is indeed an impressive selection, and they are delicious. The caramel and hazel cup is excellent. Price: 850 BF/kg, 900 BF for manons and orangettes, 800 BF for truffles.

# Dossche

61, Landjuweelsraat, 9050 Ledeberg. Tel.: 09/231.25.15.
"Making chocolate is a childhood dream, and what's more, I have been making it since I was 14 !"
Monsieur Dossche

## Background

The Dossche chocolate-making business was founded in 1968 by Etienne Dossche, and became a limited company in 1987. Everyone around Etienne Dossche who makes chocolates in the workshop has the appropriate diploma, "Suiker en chocolade bewerker".

## The Shop

The window is decorated with dolls and gift packages. The counter takes up the full length of the window, and the pralines are displayed in large boxes. The price list is fixed up behind the counter. The shop was renovated in 1997.

## The Products

The specialities are pralines, truffles and caraque (fine Venezuelan chocolate) - all, naturally, made on the premises. The pralines are large and the chocolate layer thick.
Price: 480 BF/kg.

# Druart

*13, rue de Boughors, 7387 Angreau (Honnelles).*
*Tel.: 065/75.95.21.*
*(Open: Monday-Thursday, 9.00-12.00 h and*
*14.00-17.00 h; Saturday, 10.00-12.30 h).*

*"Chocolate is a very feminine substance and if, by*
*ill-luck, I could not eat it any more myself, no*
*doubt I could not make it any more !"*
*Camille Druart*

## Background

Camille Druart gained his diploma at the Namur hotel school, with a First Prize for cooking. He gained experience in a series of prestigious restaurants: Chez Septime in Liège, and Chez Christopher and L'Ecailler du Palais Royal in Brussels, as well as in pâtisseries. He also undertook further training in "top of the range" chocolates in 1994, at the Lenôtre school. It was in 1982, after a year with a senior chocolate maker in the region, that Camille Druart's mother decided to set up a small praline workshop in their country house, to make it her hobby. In 1983 she brought her son into the

business. He requested some months to think about it, and travelled in China. It was there that he had his first stroke of fortune - in Beijing he met his future wife, Ma Kegeng - and his second would be on his return, for chocolate ! Today, the craftsman-chocolate manufacturer exports principally to France, but also to Arab countries and Great Britain. And, of course, he takes part in exhibitions in China !

## The Shop

The shop and the workshop are located behind a private house. The merchandise is displayed on the L-shaped counter in the public workshop area. The chocolatier Druart also uses this to show his "creation of the month', a new and temporary recipe presented for one month (praline with Kriek and cherries from the Nord, ganache with ginger and laurel-flower wine, etc.) There are various styles of package, including an exclusive Druart luxury box (red "lizard", flowers, etc.) and special packaging for feast-days. There is a smiling welcome. The packets contain a map and a location plan, particularly designed for French customers.

## The Products

Some forty hand-made pralines are on offer, with four types of white chocolate, ten milk, and most of them dark chocolate (70 per cent cocoa), but no fresh cream. The "Orangine noire" (hazelnut cream with natural orange flavour) or the "Matignon lait" (chocolate butter

cream, flavoured with rum with raisins macerated in rum) are specifically worth mentioning. There is a very good praline with cream and grated coconut in dark chocolate ("Bahia") and a very good truffle. Well worth a visit.

# Efdé

*3, rue de l'Harmonie, 4800 Verviers.*
*Tel.: 087/34.00.02. (Open: 9.00-18.30 h).*

*"Nothing in our background prepared us for this profession, for my husband was an electrician. It was an inexplicable lightning-strike - the love of chocolate !" Madame Michel*

## Background

The business was founded in 1946 by M. Fernand Defrance, from whose initials the company's name was created. For the last 20 years the business has belonged to Monsieur and Madame Michel, who were trained by M. Defrance. Their son has recently joined them in the workshop. Both the lay-out of the shop and the creation of the pralines continue the traditions established in the 1940s, to offer the greatest pleasure to customers in the Verviers region.

## The Shop

The shop is located in a commercial street in the city, famous for the quality and luxury of its boutiques. The interior design incorporates Limoges and other French porcelain, stoneware and christening presents. The praline counter displays some 50 varieties. The cartons are made up to the customer's wishes. They are made of a golden wrapping and white paper.

## The Products

All the pralines are made on the premises, as well as the wrapped chocolate. The specialities are the manons, orange marzipan and the fresh cream cups. Many of the pralines are moulded, but others are made in the old way and are irregular in shape. The fresh cream is highly appreciated by the customers. Foreign buyers are numerous (Germany, Spain, France, etc.) and special boxes are provided for postal despatch, including to warm climates such as Australia. Price: 680 BF/kg.

# Franz

*24, rue Saint-Gilles, 4000 Liège.*
*Tel.: 041/23.06.46.*
*(Open: Monday-Saturday, 9.00-18.30 h)*
*"I love chocolate, both as a consumer and as a maker. A pâtissier by training, with a love of creating, imagining, discovering new harmonies, I took an interest in chocolate and discovered in it a fascinating profession." M. Franz*

## Background

The business was founded in 1985. It employs two people for production (a pâtissier and a chocolatier-pâtissier graduate from CERIA), and two sales assistants.

## The Shop

The shop is particularly clean, the presentation of the pralines low-key. The staff know how to describe the products. The price-list on the counter is made of... chocolate ! The packets are white with the word Franz in embossed lettering.

## The Products

The coating of the manon is available in white or milk chocolate, or fondant. An excellent flaky praline. Generally, none of the pralines is very sweet, and this is their major advantage. The range includes plenty of fresh cream, a feature much appreciated by the customers.

# Galler

*39, rue de la Station, 4051 Chaudfontaine.*
*Tel.: 04/367.22.11.*

*"Chocolate" a magic word ! Say it out loud, and faces light up... Is there anyone who does not have a warm and tasty chocolate memory somewhere in his life?" Jean Galler*

## Background

Founded by Jean Galler in 1976, the Galler chocolate-making business is above all a family concern. Supplier to the Belgian royal court, Jean Galler sends his chocolates to every corner of the world: London, Tokyo, Paris... and in Belgium, there are 5 addresses for indulgence:

GALLER

Belgian chocolate

Brussels - Grand-Place, 44 rue au Beurre (open every day)
Liège: 2, rue de Pot d'Or (daily except Sunday)
Wavre: 13 rue du Commerce (Tuesday morning - Saturday evening)
Vaux-sous-Chèvremont: 30 rue C. Balthasart (daily except Sunday)

## The Shop

This was a visit to the shop in Liège. Ideally located in the heart of the "Carré", this temple of chocolate lays out its tempting features of every kind. In a superb old-style shop with a particularly welcoming atmosphere, assistants with immaculate gloves enthusiastically tell the customer about the secrets of each praline. The carton is magnificent and glossy, elegantly topped with a broad ribbon and floral decoration. The carefully designed interior lay-out makes it possible to choose from one layer or another without disturbing the pralines.

## The Products

"L'Extrême", a disc of dark ganache coated with 70 per cent chocolate, is a delight for lovers of pure chocolate. There is a magnificent manon and a praline very well-flavoured with Earl Grey. Successful and original combinations of flavours, as in the "Orient" praline, a truffle with honey and pistachios inside white chocolate. Flavoursome flaky pralines. Undoubtedly one of the country's best addresses...
Price: 890 BF/kg.

# Gartner

*296, Manebruggestraat, 2150 Borsbeek.*
*Tel.: 03/366.25.25.*
*(Open: 8.30-17.30 h).*
*A further sales outlet at Inno, Antwerp.*

## Background

Gartner's history began 50 years ago when Walter Gartner lovingly made his first praline.
Today, the business produces a single range of 60 pralines. Around 60 per cent of the annual production (250 tonnes) is delivered throughout the world by controlled temperature transport. Apart from most European countries, the most important outlets are Japan, Australia and the Arab Emirates.

## The Shop

The shop is in Inno, Antwerp. The chocolates are kept in a small refrigerated counter. The assistant makes up the carton with a glove, and gives the required explanations with a smile. The prices are clearly indicted, but there is no information on the contents of the pralines.

## The Products

The unusual shapes arouse curiosity. There are few moulded pralines, most are shaped from liquid chocolate and finished and decorated by hand. The shapes of the "Vatel" and the "Truffe Glacée" are very unusual. The great variety of items using a cream base is remarkable: there

GARTNER

Belgian chocolate

are a dozen, with flavours as varied as whisky, caramel, chestnut purée, and almonds. In this range, many consist of cups decorated with chocolate and flaked almonds.

The two varieties of Gianduja, one with almonds and the other with hazelnuts, are wrapped in very striking style.

The range of truffles is equally remarkable. The "Sabayon" truffle is original. It is rare to find marzipan with white chocolate on sale in Belgium, here it is enhanced with preserved pineapple.

The orangettes have an excellent flavour, and are available in dark and milk chocolate.

# Gillet

*4, Place Reine-Astrid, 1090 Brussels.*
*Tel.: 02/425.31.20.*
*(Open: Wednesday - Saturday, 9.00-19.00 h)*

*"I struck out in 1981 for this black jewel !"*
*Claude Gillet*

## Background

It was at Easter 1981 that Claude Gillet launched out in his turn into the craftsman's world of chocolate, when he bought the business founded by his grandfather in 1923 and subsequently managed by his father.

## The Shop

In the same square of shops in Jette there are other great names in chocolate. The shop is clean and fresh, and the assistant uses a glove to serve. The carton is white.

## The Products

The white chocolate manon is placed on a disc of marzipan. The coffee manon with fondant sugar is very good. Both include a white cream "enriched" with butter. Price: 1,180 BF/kg.

# Godiva

*5, rue de l'Armistice, 1081 Brussels.*
*Tel.: 02/422.17.11.*

## Background

Pierre Draps began to make pralines for the big stores in 1929. In 1946 his son Joseph, with his wife Gabrielle, created the Godiva brand, foreseeing the demand for luxury which would sweep the world after the Second World War. In 1958 Godiva opened in the rue Saint-Honoré in Paris, and in 1966 on Fifth Avenue in New York. Godiva has sales points throughout the world - its own shops, franchises, or "Shop in a Shop", as in Harrods in London or Saks in the United States. Godiva can be found in almost every Duty Free airport shop in the world. Its turnover stands at one billion BF, with 60 % from exports.

GODIVA

Belgian chocolate

## The Shop

This is at 22 Grand-Place, 1000 Brussels (Tel.: 02/511.25.37. Open: daily, 9.00-22.00 h, and from 10.00 on Sundays), no doubt Godiva's grandest sales outlet. It also displays the archetypal "Godiva" style: the colours are gold and black, the counters panoramic, the cartons an exclusive design. This shop is very popular with visiting tourists, who find sumptuous seasonal packages here and assorted pralines for gifts which are always freshly imaginative. There is also a range of prepacked assortments, securely packaged for travelling, which offer purchases at all prices and for all occasions.

## The Products

Very fine presentation, consisting of a large number of enrobed pralines. Among the moulded versions, many do not have a flat base: a double shape enables the combination of different flavours. The Godiva pralines are known for their well-defined chocolate flavour (50 per cent cocoa in the fondant, and more than 70 per cent for the extra dark !). The weight of the pralines varies between 5 and 15 grammes, with the manon weighing around 26 g. Some of the enrobed pralines consist of several layers of different chocolates. Price: 1,190 BF/kg.

# Goossens

*6, Isabellalei. 2018 Antwerp.*
*Tel.: 03/239.13.10.*
*(Open: Monday - Saturday, 8.30-18.30 h).*

*"I love this job because chocolate has no limits: creation, entertainment, flavours, presentation... And that's why I am in love with my work".*
*Erik Goossens*

## Background

The Goossens chocolate-making business has been in existence since 1955. René Goossens was the director and master chocolatier for 40 years, until his son Erik took over in 1991. René Goossens was also a teacher (CMO) in Antwerp, President of the FENACO (the Belgian national federation of master chocolate-makers and confectioners) and member of various judging panels such as for Intersuc in Paris or for the European Club.

## The Shop

A long, narrow, air-conditioned shop. The assistant uses a glove. Her advice is sound, and she is friendly. The prices of the pralines are clearly indicated, with a full list on the counter in addition, giving useful information. The cartons are claret colour.

## The Products

Among the pralines, specialities are the "diamant candisé", "palets de Rubens", "étoile européenne" and "Fabiolet".

The master chocolate-maker is also the creator of "Antwerpsch Handjes", "Logos", and others. The moulded pralines are decorated with pouch or cornet. The praline *en croûte* with liqueur is excellent. Various items made of marzipan and chocolate are shaped according to the need of the moment. Chocolate sculpture items are also available. Price: 1,180 BF/kg.

# Irsi

*15, rue de Bailli, 1050 Brussels.*
*Tel.: 02/648.70.50. (Open: Monday-Saturday,*
*8.30-19.00 h Also, run by Monsieur Corne's*
*daughter-in-law, at: 176, Chaussée de Bruxelles,*
*1410 Waterloo. Tel.: 02/354.66.21).*

*"My work has always been as part of the family.*
*I am very proud at seeing my children following*
*their father's profession ! One reason, apart from*
*a passion for chocolate, is that I have never*
*complained to any of them about the inevitable*
*drawbacks of this trade, but always talked about*
*its attractive aspects. I think that that is a good*
*way to transmit one's own enthusisam."*
*Norbert Corne.*

## Background
Founded in 1926, the business has always remained at the same address. It is a family company, run today by Monsieur and Madame Norbert Corne-Dupont, their two sons Florent and Jean-Marie, and their daughter Marie-Anne.

## The Shop
The shop, which is air-conditioned, stands in a very lively district, popular with young people and artists. It is designed to look like an old traditional house, in the style of an English sweet-shop. The shelves and display cases hold porcelain pieces and various decorative gift articles, as well as an enormous range of christening presents, with the prices indicated.

## The Products
A vast range to choose from, of more than 70 different pralines, as well as house specialities: six kinds of manons and pralines made with fresh cream. Their home-made fruit pastes have a display counter all to themselves. For customers in a hurry, ready-prepared cartons are on sale, containing an assortment of home-made pralines. One of the best Belgian praline houses. Price: 960 BF/kg.

# Laubach

*17, rue du Postillon, 1180 Brussels (Uccle).*
*Tel.: 02/346.22.52.*
*(Open: Monday-Saturday, 9.30-28.30h).*

*"I have had an overwhelming passion for chocolate since my youngest childhood. There is never a day when I don't eat a piece of chocolate. The wish to set up shop and express myself is nothing new for me: it is the result of all those years of experience..." Francis Laubach*

## Background

The shop was opened in 1993... on 1 April ! It is run by Monsieur and Madame Francis Laubach; he gained his experience through working for 20 years in a famous pâtisserie in the Avenue Louise.

## The Shop

This is a pretty little shop devoted entirely to chocolate. The prices are shown. The handsome carton is white, printed in gold, with a blue ribbon. At the back of the shop, M. Francis Laubach's workshop is visible behind the shop, with the marble, the tempering machine, the moulds, etc.

## The Products

The range extends to 62 different pralines. The white chocolate is very good, as is the truffle between two layers of nougatine. The rum and raisin ganache is very successful, and the cherry in kirsch is excellent. There is a good balance between fresh creams, ganaches, pralines and fondants. The diabetic chocolate, in white, dark or milk, on sale in bars, is worth noting. Price: 980 BF/kg.

# Maison Léger

*Olivier, Pierre and Renaud Léger*
*55, rue de la Station, 7850 Enghien.*
*Tel/Fax: 02/395.38.74.*
*on sale also at "Sucré-Salé",*
*24A, rue E. Cambier, 7800 Ath.*
*(Open: Tuesday-Saturday: 9.00-19.00 h,*
*Sunday: 10.00-13.00h).*

## Background

The Léger brothers' adventure began in their mother's kitchen. In 1994, all three of them trained engineers, they decided to pool their individual talents. With the memory of his final studies on "the sensorial analysis of chocolate", Olivier arranged to meet a large number of experienced chocolate makers, which was how his passion became clear. High quality products demand costly materials. Next came Renaud, the youngest brother, who developed a tempering machine by putting together a stainless steel vat, a computer... and a good deal of ingenuity. This item now has a place in the family museum, yielding its place to more professional equipment. The people of Enghien were increasingly attracted and Pierre, the oldest, joined the business to oversee the administrative and financial sides.

## The Shop

The shop is arranged with taste round antique furniture in a private house. It lies slightly out of the city centre. The classic carton (a "special" for feast-days) is green, blue or claret gingham, and the closure is decorated with a small flower chosen by the customer from a basket on the counter. A folder explains the contents and gives advice to the interested customer.

## The Products

Two pots of chocolate spread are available: 280 ml or an individual pot, 30 ml. There are twelve varieties of chocolate batons (for which the wrapping can be personalised): white coconut, dark praline, etc. The "Special dark Maison Léger" is very dark ! The filling often consists of three layers: chocolate, praline, chocolate. As for the pralines with distinctive names - "la spirale", "la dame", "le hérisson" ("hedgehog") etc., the best are undoubtedly the ones made with fresh cream and with Grand-Marnier ganache. Price: 680 BF/kg.

# Jean-Loup Legrand

*19, place du Monument, 4900 Spa.*
*Tel.: 087/77.13.56.*
*(Open: Tuesday - Sunday, 9.00-12.30 h*
*and 14.00-18.30).*

*"My passion for chocolate developed over time, particularly for working with chocolate and the opportunity to create something unique." Jean-Loup Legrand*

## Background

The pâtisserie was founded in 1980, and also made pralines. The shop opened in 1987, and is devoted entirely to chocolate.

## The Shop

The shop is located in the centre of Spa, with its workshop visible behind the shop through the glass doors and panels.

## The Products

There are truffles here, and fruit - orangettes, citronettes, pineapple quarters, cerisettes. But also, of course, pralines: with liqueurs, with local specialities in particular: pralines with Spa elixir, and with Houyeux Pékèt. Nut and fruit *mendiants* at 900 BF/kg and batons at 30 Bf each. The range of other items includes Easter eggs, Christmas logs, clogs, boxes and St Nicolas items, according to season; and special personal commissions are also available.
Price: 940 BF/kg.

# Mahieu

*4 place Dumon, 1150 Stockel.*
*Tel.: 02/772.72.45.*
*(Open: Tuesday - Friday, 7.30-19.00; Saturday,*
*7.00-19.00 h, and Sunday, 7.00-13.00 h).*

*"The creation of the chocolate department was for*
*us a logical consequence of the steady expansion of*
*our business and of our research for quality pro-*
*ducts. Personalising our chocolates was also a way*
*of establishing us firmly in this sector, so that our*
*customers could deal with all their confectionery*
*purchases within a single establishment."*
*Freddy Mahieu*

## Background

The pâtisserie was founded by Monsieur and
Madame Freddy Mahieu in 1978. Today, the
staff numbers 40 people.

## The Shop

The pralines are presented in an area at the centre
of the pâtisserie shop. The counter is made of air-
conditioned green marble and faced with glass. A
dozen members of staff look after the shop, and
orders. The assistants are smiling and competent
and serve their customers with a throw-away transparent plastic glove. The décor is dark and quiet.

## The Products

Naturally, there is plenty of pâtisserie. On the
praline side there is a sound balance between
coated and moulded items. There is no white
praline; the pralines are small. There are not
many ganaches, and no fresh cream. An excellent address. Price: 1,075 BF/kg.

# Léonidas

*43, Boulevard J.-Graindor, 1070 Brussels.*
*Tel.: 02/522.19.57.*

## Background

Léonidas Kestekidès, the founder, rewarded in
1913 by the Gold Medal at the Ghent Universal
Exhibition in which he participated, and retained by a beautiful Brussels girl whom he married, settled in Belgium and opened his first
shops in Brussels, Ghent and Blankenberghe. In
1935 the legendary shop opened in the Boulevard Anspach in Brussels, facing the street,
where customers could buy pralines - at a
modest price and chosen loose - which are
famous for their quality and freshness. In addition to the first factory, which faced the Brussels
stock exchange, a second and a third were established in Anderlecht in 1983 and 1993, proof
of a company in good health, with a turn over of
around 3 billion francs. Léonidas produces two-
thirds of Belgian pralines, on sale at 1,750 sales
points throughout the world, including 535 in
France, for example in Paris, Marseille, Toulou-
se, Antibes, Bordeaux, Nice, Calais, Charlevil-
le-Mézières, Dijon, Grenoble, Cognac, Lyon,
Limoges, Nantes, Perpignan and Strasbourg. The
maximum price is 148 French francs per kilo.

LÉONIDAS

## The Shop

The visit was to the legendary shop at 46 boulevard Anspach, 1000 Brussels (tel: 02/218.03.63. Open: daily, 9.00-19.00h; Sunday, 10.00-18.00h). The lighting is diffuse, two large crystal chandeliers are set above the work-table. The large counter is open onto the street, along about ten metres of the façade. The sales assistants' uniform is the traditional yellow apron. All wear a glove on their right hand.

## The Products

Léonidas pralines are the most widely sold in Belgium. Apart from the traditional range which comprises 83 varieties of praline, Léonidas makes caramels, chocolate shells and fruits de mer, pure liqueurs, figurines, hollow chocolate items for garnishing, and seasonal items. The famous Léonidas manon, covered with white chocolate, invented and launched by the company in the 1980s, has come to replace the classic manon made of fondant sugar in Belgium. Price: 460 BF/kg.

# Marcolini

*137, avenue Reine-Astrid, 1950 Kraainem.
Tel.: 02/721.24.71.
(Open: Monday-Saturday, 10.00-12.30 h, 14.00-18.30 h, Sunday, 10.00-13.00 h).
Place Witchers, 75 M, Avenue Louise,
1050 Brussels. (Open: Monday-Saturday,
10.00-18.30 h).*

*39, Place du Grand-Sablon, 1000 Brussels.
Tel.: 02/514.12.06. (Open: Tuesday-Sunday,
10.00-19.00 h).
137, avenue du X-Septembre, Luxembourg.
Tel.: 352.45.29.60.*

*"In my eyes, chocolate is one of the most noble substances in existence. But quality can only be achieved by combining the generosity of the land with human talent... which is where the craftsman comes in. I have had the good fortune to practice a profession which gives pleasure to other people... Nothing is ever taken for granted in this trade, where every day the chocolatier has to find the right balance between the blend of flavours and his search for the right taste."*
*Pierre Marcolini*

## Background

In 1992 Pierre Marcolini opened the Sugar Design School at Kraainem, to teach the sugar decoration of pâtisserie. In August 1994 he settled in the Avenue Reine-Astrid at Kraainem and with his wife Nicolette Regout opened a shop next to the workshops.

## The Shop

The shop lies at the heart of a residential area and attracts a knowledgeable clientèle. Behind a bay window part of the workshop can be seen in action. On the shelving behind the very long counter, other top-of-the-range products are also on show, such as jams and other conserves. A substantial range of pralines is on display. The gloved assistants

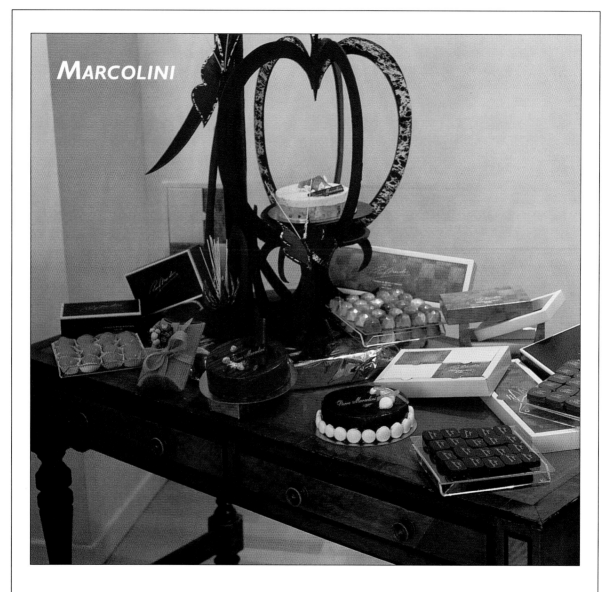

MARCOLINI

make up the cartons to the customer's wishes; the box itself is made of corrugated card or a wide selection of distinctive boxes, a style which contrasts strongly with the classic packaging.

## The Products

Pierre Marcolini has created 70 different varieties of praline. Pralines with flavours as diverse as tea, cinnamon and violets. He uses a coating chocolate which is not too rich, long in the mouth, its finesse retained on the palate, structured, full and round, to achieve the right flavour, as one does for a good wine. In particular he has specialised in working with bitter chocolate. He skilfully makes use of all the diversity of the beans from various origins. And the care is justified ! A small proportion of pralines is made with liqueur, of which we consider the best to be the rum and raisin ganache. The pralines are small and average in size, which makes them very pleasant to eat. Price 1,400 BF/kg. Pierre Marcolini is famous for the gâteau with which he carried off the world cup for pâtisserie at Lyon in 1995; it consists of an orange crème brûlée and a mousse made of bitter dark chocolate. Certainly one of our finest craftsmen. In addition, Marcolini offers customers themed evenings with tastings (such as chocolate, wine, spices, etc.). Another way of satisfying the public's gourmet interests.

# Mary

*73, rue Royale, 1000 Brussels.*
*Tel.: 02/217.45.00.*
*(Open: Tuesday-Saturday, 9.00-18.00 h).*
*"We are in this business because we love it !"*
*Madame Lamberty*

## Background

The shop was founded in 1919 by Mademoiselle Mary Delluc. She offered "chocolate sweets' from a pre-1900 recipe book. Queen Elisabeth of the Belgians granted her the official title of Supplier to the Court. For town planning reasons Monsieur and Madame Lamberty, the present-day owners, had to move recently to No. 73 in the same rue Royale. They recall the days before the war when no fewer than ten assistants were busy behind the gilded counters, serving ambassadors and chairmen from the United States who were visiting Brussels.

## The Shop

The design of the shop recalls the great "Mary" tradition. Customers can admire carved wooden boxes designed for communions and christenings, decorated with a reproduction of hand-painting dating from the beginning of the century.

## The Products

The range consists of more than 70 different fillings, prepared in traditional moulds. The "Mary" was created ten years ago, a praline with a slender flake of nougatine and the name inscribed in gold. The bitter chocolate mousse is highly recommended. The 150g box of caraque chocolates (99.7 per cent cocoa solids) costs 202 BF.

# Mireille

*"Chocolatier de la Gileppe"*
*14, rue Hauglustaine, 4834 Limbourg-Goé*
*Tel.: 087/76.23.68.*
*(Open: Monday-Friday, 8.00-17.00h).*

*"I was practially born into this business. The pleasure of creating treats which chocolate lovers taste and enjoy gives us enormous pleasure..." Mireille Werts*

## Background

Praline making started in 1966 under Madame Berthe Darimont, mother of the present-day director Mireille Werts, who runs it with her husband Claude Carpentier. Sales outlets: Les Délices de Mireille in Verviers, Le Chocolat Gourmand in Liège, La Marquisette in Grâce-Hollogne, La Pralinette in La Calamine, La Gourmandine in Welkenraedt, and Le Palais de la Praline at Aubel, as well as a large number of bakeries and pâtisseries in the Liège area.

## The Shop

We visited the "Les Délices de Mireille", a sales outlet in the "Nouveau-Bazar" in Verviers (Tel.: 087/31.66.17). The brand is visible and attracts attention. The counter offers a good selection. The price is indicated. The box is yellow.

## The Products

Specialities: champagne truffles, "Prestige" pralines (praline, plain and hazelnut fresh cream), liqueurs, 20 kinds of filled eggs, the "Farodine" (orange and almond flavoured marzipan), the "Paola" (butter cream, moka, almonds), whisky truffles... Mireille also offers spreads, batons and hollow chocolates.

# Mondose

*2, Postweg, 1602 Vlezenbeek.*
*Tel.: 02/568.22.11.*

## Background

In 1978 the brothers Jean-Jacques and Claude Poncelet took over the management of Neuhaus and amalgamated it with the Mondose brand. Today, Neuhaus-Mondose, which forms part of the Artal group, produces 2,000 tonnes of pralines annually, exported to 36 countries.

## The Shop

We visited the shop "Le Chocolatier" at 80 rue du Progrès (CNN), 1030 Brussels.
Tel.: 02/203.28.49. (Open: 7.30-18.00h).

The chocolatier shows sound knowledge of the hand-made pralines that he sells. The shop is open and modern. In an attractive setting, your selection is arranged in the carton. The carton itself is beige and claret-coloured.

## The Products

The pralines are available in the usual varieties, from the manon to the *mendiant*. The general quality is good. Mondose makes pralines, chocolate bars and batons, and also a whole series of seasonal chocolate items: small filled Easter eggs, large decorated eggs, Christmas sabots and large Saint-Nicolas figures, or other designs which are all impressive accompaniments for festival occasions (Christmas, Valentine's Day, Easter, etc.). Approximate price: 850 BF/kg.

# Neuhaus

2, Postweg, 1602 Vlezenbeek.
Tel.: 02/568.22.11.

*"Settle yourself down in a light restful place, relax. Place your praline delicately into your mouth and let it melt for a few moments. Taste it three or four times, and discover the delicate flavour of the blend between the filling and the exterior. Assess the length in the mouth and awaken the sensation which only experience will enable you to develop."*
Jean Neuhaus

## Background

The firm of Neuhaus is one of the oldest in the country. Further, Jean Neuhaus was the inventor of the "praline" in 1912, and of the "ballotin", (the classic container for Belgian pralines), with his wife Louise Agostini, in 1915. His son-in-law, Adelson De Gavre, managed the firm from 1923 onwards. After various take-overs in the late 1970s, Neuhaus also took on Mondose and Corné Port-Royal. From 1989 the company has held the major part of the "Jeff de Bruges" company in Paris. Neuhaus produces 2,000 tonnes per year, and exports to 36 countries. In Belgium, Neuhaus goods are on sale in 52 shops (of which a dozen belong to the company), in 100 sales-points in pâtisseries and in 400 shops in Germany, 200 in the United States and 72 in Japan.

## The Shop

We visited the shop at 35 rue Archimède, 1040 Brussels (open: Monday-Friday, 9.00-18.30h, and Saturday, 9.00-13.00h). The shop is superb, welcoming and decorated in Neuhaus style. Cartons are kept ready made up behind the counter. Gloves are always used. The prices are well indicated. The name of the pralines is indicated before each item of information. The carton has two colours, green and gold; this has become legendary, as has the "N" of Neuhaus, in use since the company was formed.

## The Products

Neuhaus offers more than 70 different pralines in its assortment. There are established selections: "Opéra", "Bruxelles" (a single type of chocolate in little boxes), "Boîtes en fer" ... When the carton is opened, the moulded pralines are visible next to the coated pralines in a pleasing arrangement. Some, even finer, are presented in paper cups.

NEUHAUS

Belgian chocolate

Their weight may vary between 9 and 15 g. We have a weakness for "Tentation", pralines made entirely by hand: nougatine, fresh cream, coffee, and, for the "Bonbon 13", almond ganache flavoured with rum.

# Nihoul

*192, Chaussée de Vleurgat, 1050 Brussels.*
*Tel.: 02/626.90.30.*

## Background

In 1896 Louis Nihoul founded a family business in the rue Neuve. In 1910 he moved to the Avenue Louise, supported by his son Léon Nihoul and, later, by his grandson Christian Nihoul who he had trained himself in creating emulsions. Surrounded by the delicate scents of chocolate making, fascinated from his youngest days by the magic and the aromas of the materials, inspired by graphic arts, Christian Nihoul set out to become one of the finest ambassadors for Belgian chocolate; he is often its protagonist at gastronomic festivals (New York, Moscow, Beirut), in television programmes or at conferences. For great occasions he has created gâteaux which remain celebrated. In May 1997 he founded Gourmand Gaillard, a new business in his own image, a few metres away from the premises in the Avenue Louise which closed in July 1997.

## The Shop

In a setting of light-coloured woods, Gourmand Gaillard is fully open from dawn with breakfasts, snacks and lunch menus created round seasonal materials, the pâtisserie which has made Christian Nihoul famous and for which he constantly and enthusiastically creates new variations, and his famous specially created chocolates. With a wine list which judiciously promotes a few wine producers of the new generation, there may be tasting evenings with chocolates, wines and porto, and those leaving this open-hearted location often do so with a charming little chocolate ballotin in the hand.

## The Products

Constantly researched, the new pralines from Christian Nihoul are smaller than previously. He has also recently introduced new flavours into his range of fillings, such as ginger. But for the purists he still offers a bitter chocolate ganache, and his classic range is still available for the faithful clientèle which has followed him. Price: 1,250 BF/kg.

# Passion chocolat

*197, rue Père-E.-Devroye, 1150 Brussels.*
*Tel/Fax: 02/772.47.10.*
*(Open, Tuesday-Thursday, 10.00-15.00 h and 17.00-19.00 h. Friday, to 20.00 h. Saturdays, 10.00-18.00 h).*

*"My thanks to you, my friend Praline, for the well-being that you bring me. For many years you have shared my joys and my troubles. Your ever-faithful discreet presence on the corner of a table or by my bed, or on my desk, gave me at every mouthful that*

little "lift" which is so precious. Your "something extra which makes all the difference" goes with me today in this mad wish which took hold of me, to set out in a new direction... Our fates seem linked for life, and I delight in it." Clare Macq.

## Background

Yet another fine love story: Claire Macq, secretary, is passionate about chocolate. She pursues the dream of becoming a chocolate maker while training at CERIA. In December 1996 she opens a boutique in the salon of her own house and installs her workshop in the basement.

## The Shop

A pretty little house near the College of Saint-Michel thus becomes the setting for this "passion" for chocolate. A wistaria grows up the green and yellow façade. Inside, Claire Macq displays and explains her creations with warmth and efficiency. The carton of hand-made pralines is perfect: it is a little chest, claret coloured, secured with a ribbon, straw and flowers which give it a very pleasing rustic air. A slip of paper inside indicates the date the contents were packed, their ingredients, and how to look after them. Perfection !

## The Products

The cartons of pralines can be "mini" (55-110 BF), or up to 1 kg (850 BF). There are also fruit pastes (orange, pear, blackcurrant, raspberry, passion-fruit and lemon) and bars of chocolate with 72 per cent cocoa solids (750 BF/kg). Two products are more original still: a series of reproductions of the bas-relief of the temple of Khajuraho, in India, showing... poses from the Kama Sutra (295 BF), and a "chocolate message" on a gianduja base, at 25 BF per letter. When imagination and talent get together, anything is possible... !

# Pâtisserie Pierre Alain

10, Grand Place, 7700 Mouscron.
Tel.: 056/34.80.24. Fax: 056/34.08.18.
(Open: Tuesday-Sunday, 7.00-20.00 h).
Other addresses: Pâtisserie DAL, 6, rue du Gaz,
7700 Mouscron; Pâtisserie Pierre-Alain,
10, rue d'Audenaerde. 7730 Estaimpuis.

"Chocolate, like wine, is a noble product which should be tasted in a state of mind associating the warmth of life and the physical well-being."
Pierre-Alain

## Background

The business was established in 1965 by Francis Gabriels. His son, Pierre-Alain, followed his example in taking advanced training in chocolate-making at Locle in Switzerland. The Dalandière chocolate making business is outstanding in its creation of some original and unusual products.

## The Shop

Norman in style and completely renovated, the main shop stands at the centre of the Grand-Place at the heart of Mouscron. The legendary welcome of the Picardy and border regions is clearly present, as much in the pâtisserie as in the refreshment room.

## The Products

In 1970 the establishment created the chocolate "Hurlu", the insubordinate symbol of the city, carved by a Swiss craftsman. It was moulded in caraque chocolate with praline filling. In 1980, it was the "Pavé", moulded in dark, milk and white praline, which appeared, representing this time the famous pavé streets of the Nord. And recently, a chocolate "Frite" has appeared, which has been patented and put on sale. It is of course presented in a twist of paper ! This very unusual chocolate was kept for a competition organised by the Conseil Régional du Nord, in Lille. There is also an assortment of pralines (including excellent mendiants), presented in a white carton, wrapped in yellow flowered paper and tied with a tartan ribbon and a little bunch of flowers, for the finest effect ! Price, 800 BF/kg.

# Sweertvaegher

*17, Korte Steenstraat, 8500 Kortrijk.*
*Tel.: 056.22.23.49.*

## Background

The Sweertvaegher chocolate factory was founded in 1933 at Ypres. Monsieur Sweertvaegher having retired from business shortly after the company's fiftieth birthday, the present-day director is Jan

Verougstraete. Branches: 3, Neermarkt, Ieper; 29 Philipstockstraat, Bruges; 16 Schuttershofstraat, Antwerp;, and 27 Mageleinstraat, Ghent.

## The Shop

We visited the shop at 15 Schuttershofstraat, 2000 Antwerp (Tel.: 03/226.36.91. Open: Monday-Saturday, 9.30-18.30h and Sunday, 10.00-24.00h) The air-conditioned shop is plain and simple and very light. The pralines are laid out in wicker baskets, very effectively. The prices are clearly shown on the counter, but there is no label to show the contents of the pralines.

## The Products

A good balance between moulded, coated and hand-shaped pralines. No white chocolate. The marzipan, with a good flavour of almonds, is a little too sweet. The very flat praline filled with praline, with the company's coat of arms, is a real treat ! (Price: 880 BF/kg)

# Ten Ryen

*Ten Ryen sprl, 86, place Eugène Keym,*
*1170 Brussels. Tel.: 02/675.35.82.*
*(Open: 10.00-19.00h, except Sunday).*

*"Every day we must confirm our ability to respond to the very reasonable demands of our customers. Is it not said that chocolate is the nectar of the gods? And have you ever seen anyone eating chocolate with a gloomy expression?" Michel Van Doorslaer*

## Background

The shop was established in September 1994 in the commercial heart of Watermael-Boitsfort. The name chosen by Michel Van Doorslaer is that of a place in Flanders, a site linked with his own family history.

## The Shop

The prettily coloured shop with attractive design is one of the highlights of the shopping gallery. It offers pralines in a coloured kraft carton, with the blue logo stamped firmly on it.

## The Products

Most of the production comes to this shop. In its pralines, the business follows the strong current trends, such as ganaches and pralines. But there is a praline mixture which is different from the others, and this particular flavour appears to attract a faithful clientèle. The owner has no wish to become the "King of truffles" or the "Emperor of manons": his ambition is to satisfy all tastes: that of marzipan lovers as much as the faithful followers of fresh cream. The customer is always right in his selection. A business worth encouraging. Price: 980 BF/kg.

# *Wittamer*®

6, 12, 13 place du Grand-Sablon, 1000 Brussels.
Tel.: 02/512.37.42. Fax: . 02/512.52.09.
E-mail: Wittamer @ Wittamer.be
(Open: daily, 7.00-19.00h).

*"Two minutes away, Edouard ran round to Wittamer and ate eight tiny coffee éclairs. For eight minutes he believed that God had created the world."* Pascal Quignard, Les Escaliers de Chambord (NRF, Gallimard)

## Background

Wittamer entered history in Le Sablon in 1910. Henri Wittamer, of Austrian origins and born in Arlon, was the founder of the business. On his death in 1945, his only son Henri-Gustave and his wife Yvonne took the future of the name in hand: bakery, patisserie, and tea-rooms are the key features. They it was who in the 1960s, with the help of their son Henri-Paul, were at the foundations of a veritable culinary revolution: the introduction into the range of traditional confectionery of the new patisserie. It was also Henri-Paul who, following his student days in Switzerland, set up the "chocolaterie" department, the logical development which responded to the demands of their customers. His sister Myriam joined the company in 1980. Her role was in public relations and new products. She introduced a catering section (shop, receptions and business catering), took on the confectionery which expanded, and broke into new territory such as gourmet gifts sent as far as Australia, and exports. In 1985 Wittamer was once more ahead

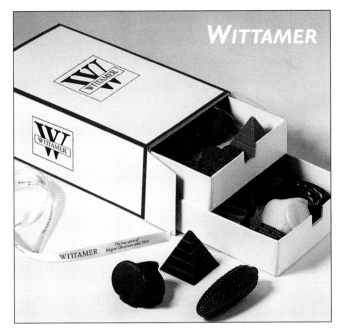

# WITTAMER

visible at the rear, separated by a glass screen. Behind the main counter, three metres long, stand the white-clad assistants, transparent gloves on their right hands. Labels identify each item, and the prices are clearly shown.

## The Products

Among others: the sweets, "Astrid", consisting of an orange mousse with chocolate filling, created in honour of the marriage of their Royal Highnesses Prince Lorenz and Princess Astrid of Belgium; and "Samba", two mousses made of contrasting chocolates. This gâteau won the Prix Valrhona in June 1986, a prize awarded to a member of the prestigious international society "Relais Desserts"; *Pain au chocolat* filled with a double bar of bitter chocolate; "chocolate in every style", a selection plate consisting essentially of chocolate, served in the tea-rooms; bitter chocolate truffle, the great hit; the sweet "St Idesbald" which is part of the series of culturally-inspired special-occasion gâteaux which Wittamer likes to create for this type of event. This particular creation was invented with the help of the royal Fine Arts museum, in honour of the Paul Delvaux retrospective. It consists of a "back to tradition" gâteau: chocolate mousse, light biscuit, airy meringue. Currently being planned: the gâteau which will celebrate the René Magritte retrospective (spring 1998).

of fashion and changed its packaging image: like the products, it was deliberately colourful, fresh and innovative. In 1994 Leslie Wittamer, the founder's great-grand-daughter, took over "Les Salons et les Terrasses du Sablon" while her cousin Isabelle specialised in the company's finances. Autumn 1997: introduction of the "Worldwide®" carton, designed to be despatched by special delivery anywhere in the world. The Wittamer saga continues...

## The Shop

The shops are superb, plain and light. Marble is used with fine timber. Part of the workshop is

*Chocolate
and sauce*

# V. A passion for chocolate

Recipes using chocolate.
Matching chocolate with wine.
Five gastronomic critics
and their love affair
with Belgian chocolate.

# Recipes with chocolate

(French and Belgian recipes indicate crème fraîche; if this is not available, use double cream instead.)

## Chocolate Mousse
- Ingredients
150 g dark chocolate
150 g fresh cream
2 eggs

- Method
Bring the fresh cream to the boil.
Add the chocolate, in small pieces.
Whisk for about 3 minutes.
Add the egg yolks.
Whip the whites till firm and add them to the mixture.

## Chocolate Truffles
-Ingredients
200 g butter
400 g hazelnut spread
250 g dark chocolate

-Method
Soften the butter, add the softened hazelnut spread and then the chocolate, warmed to 35°.
Mould into balls of the required size, put in the fridge.
After chilling, dip into melted chocolate then roll in cocoa or powdered chocolate.

## Chocolate Biscuit Cake
- Ingredients
6 eggs
170 g caster sugar
180 g flour
30 g cocoa
40 g butter

- Method
Beat the eggs and sugar together over a very low flame until the contents reach 40°.
Take off the heat, add the melted butter, then the sieved flour and cocoa.
Blend very gently.
Pour into a mould and bake in the oven at 200° for 25 minutes.
Check by pricking with a knife point: if the blade remains clean, the biscuit is done. Leave it to cool completely, then cover this base with ganache cream at 28°. Chill.

## Ganache
- Ingredients
500 g dark chocolate cut into pieces
500 g fresh cream
150 g glucose

- Method
Bring the fresh cream and glucose to the boil. Add the chocolate in pieces and blend until it is fully melted.

## Chocolate sauce
- Ingredients
100 g dark chocolate
150 g fresh cream

- Method
Bring the fresh cream to the boil and add the chocolate

Chocolate mousse.

in small pieces. Blend until all the chocolate is melted. Serve.

### Chocolate Ice Cream

- Ingredients
1 l milk
35 g cocoa powder
8 eggs
150 g sugar
200 g fresh cream
250 g dark chocolate

- Method
Grate the chocolate finely.

Blend and heat the milk with the cocoa and 50 g sugar. In a separate bowl, mix 7 egg yolks with one whole egg and 100 g sugar.
Whisk to a mousse-like consistency.
Pour a little of the hot chocolate milk on to the egg mixture, stir, cook gently like custard, stirring without boiling.
When it coats the spoon, take off the heat, add the grated chocolate and the cream.
Whisk and mix.
Put ice-cubes into a bowl and pour on the chocolate cream.
Whisk until it is cold.
Pour the chilled cream into a sorbet-maker to freeze.

*Mendiants.*

## Mendiants

*(The mendiant is a selection of dried fruit set in melted chocolate. Its name is derived from the colour of the robes of the four mendicant orders: white for the Dominicans, violet for the Augustinians, grey for the Franciscans and brown for the Carmelites.)*

- Ingredients
500 g dark chocolate
100 g praline, made with almonds and hazelnuts
500 g nuts and dried fruit: toasted hazelnuts and almonds, shelled pistachios, raisins, preserved orange peel

- Method
Mix the nuts and dried fruit.

Chop the dark chocolate into small pieces, and melt it in a bain-marie, stirring gently.
When the chocolate is melted, mix it completely with the praline.
Pour onto a metal sheet between metal borders.
Add the fruit and nut mixture, spreading and pressing it gently into the chocolate while it is still hot.
Chill in the fridge for several minutes.
Cut into squares.

## Chocolate Parfait
- Ingredients
125 g dark and milk chocolate, in small pieces
Icing sugar
3 egg yolks

20 cl fresh cream
1 packet of vanilla sugar

- Method
Melt the chocolate over low heat in three tablespoons of water, add the sugar and blend it in. Incorporate the 3 egg-yolks and put to chill in the fridge.
Put the fresh cream into a large bowl, add the vanilla sugar and beat until smooth.
Add the cooled chocolate and mix.
Put in the freezer.
Take out 15 minutes before serving.

## Chocolate Fondue (for 6)
- Ingredients
300 g chocolate
25 cl fresh cream
50 g butter
150 g crushed hazelnuts
3 bananas
3 pears
3 mandarin oranges
6 slices of cake
Assortment of dried fruit
Milk
Lemon juice

- Method
Prepare all the fruit in slices and pieces.
Sprinkle with lemon juice to prevent browning.
Arrange on a plate.
Put the crushed hazelnuts into small individual bowls. Melt the chocolate with 2 tablespoons of milk in a casserole dish heated in a bain-marie.
Whisk in the fresh cream, then blend in the butter and sugar.

Put the casserole on the heater, set on the table.
Dip the pieces of fruit in with forks, then roll them in the nuts.

## Crème au chocolat (for 6)
- Ingredients
200 g chocolate
75 cl milk
6 egg yolks
80 g sugar
40 g cornflour

- Method
Pour 10 cl of boiling milk onto the chocolate, broken into small pieces, until it melts.
Blend the cornflour with 10 cl of milk.
In a large bowl, whisk the sugar and egg yolks until the mixture turns white, then blend in the cornflour and the chocolate milk while it is still warm.
Whisking all the time, bring to the boil and a creamy consistency. Cool, then chill in the fridge.

## Vanilla and Chocolate Profiteroles (for 6)
- Ingredients
30 small choux puffs
75 cl vanilla ice cream
75 cl hot chocolate sauce

- Method
Put the ice-cream in the fridge to allow it to soften uniformly. Keep the sauce warm.
Cut open the choux puffs, fill them with vanilla ice cream, leaving the side open. Trickle chocolate sauce over each one and put a generous amount of sauce into the plate.

*Vanilla and chocolate profiteroles.*

## DARK CHOCOLATE

A naturally sweet wine - Tawny port or mature Banyuls
- Bitter dark chocolate
  Vintage Port or Maury
- Dark chocolate filled with dark ganache cream
  A naturally sweet wine, a very young vintage
  or a recent Rivesaltes
- Dark chocolate with Earl Grey tea filling
  Mature red wine: a fifteen-year-old Bordeaux,
  or 100 per cent Syrah of about ten years' age
- Dark chocolate with ganache and biscuit filling
  Oxydised sweet unfortified wine:
  1989 amber Rivesaltes

## MILK CHOCOLATE

Sweet white wines: straw wine or sweet sherry
- Milk chocolate with caramel or praline filling
  Light sweet white wine: Romanian Traminer,
  late vintage, 5-6 years old

- Milk chocolate with tea ganache filling
  Chardonnay from Australia or the United States
- Milk chocolate with crisp biscuit filling:
  Dry red wine made from Syrah vines
- Milk chocolate with cinnamon filling:
  Madeira
- Milk chocolate with vanilla filling:
  Chenin, late vintage from the Loire valley

## GÂTEAU, 100 per cent chocolate

Virgen Malaga or Moscatel Sherry

A particular case: chocolate gâteau with orange crème brûlée and covered with ganache - the Belgian team's gâteau for the final of the pâtisserie World Cup at Lyon in 1995: a sweet red wine, Maury du Mas Amiel Vintage 1993

(from: Eric Boschman)

## Chocolate Soufflé (for 6)
- Ingredients
150 g chocolate
6 eggs
75 g sugar
A small spoonful of powdered cinnamon
Salt, butter

- Method
Melt the chocolate in a little water until it is smooth.
Put 4 egg yolks in a bowl; keep the 6 whites in another bowl.

Add the sugar to the yolks and whisk them to a mousse. Add the chocolate and cinnamon.
Put salt into the egg-whites and beat them to a firm snow.
Mix half into the chocolate, then add the rest, stirring gently and lightly from top to bottom.
Butter an oven-proof dish.
Spread the mixture into the dish and place in the centre of the oven (preheated to 220°C).
Take out as soon as the soufflé has risen, and serve immediately.

# The "love-affair" of five gastronomic critics

PAUL WILLEMS
(PRESENTER OF GOURMANDISE ON
TV-RTBF AND COOKERY CRITIC
UNDER THE NAME OF "PROFITERO-
LE" FOR LA LIBRE BELGIQUE)

### A passion for chocolate?
I adore it, but this is not a passion in the strict sense of the word. But I adore it because it can be used as the perfect finishing touch for drinks, desserts and baked dishes. Above all I love its flavour which is exclusive - unless the law is changed - to a few products which still represent what we now call "true taste". In the 17th century Carl Linnaeus classified the cacao tree as part of the "eighteenth Candira polyadelphous" under the genus Theobromine, in other words the food of the gods. Theobromine, an extract of the cacao tree, is an azote base, an alcaloid similar to caffeine, with diuretic properties which make it a cardiovascular analeptic. This is what explains the phenomenon of habituation which some chocolate enthusiasts may observe ...

### A memory connected to chocolate?
In September 1940 I was twelve years old. School had begun again and there were still chocolate batons in the little shops near the Athénée. These were "Jacques", and we fought over them amongst friends, because they were good, sweet, melting and comforting - but also because there was a photograph in the wrapper. Very soon there was no more chocolate. I have forgotten the theme of the photos, but not the chocolate ...

### A favourite chocolate baton?
The 60 per cent fondant bitter chocolate, for the "true flavour", of course. In the order Callebaut, Galler, Delhaize.

### The three best pralines?
Among many others:
1. Wittamer's "Pralinone" : milk chocolate coating, praline cream with hazelnut flakes.
2. Wittamer's classic black truffle: dark chocolate subtly enhanced with milk chocolate.
3. Wittamer's "Hospitalène": a light coating of dark chocolate flavoured with Hospitalène, a gentle red wine from Provence.

PIETER VAN DOVEREN
(COOKERY JOURNALIST FOR KNACK
WEEK END/TRENDS)

### A passion for chocolate?
To each his preference. The love of chocolate is not hereditary - people fall in love with chocolate, and then the desire for chocolate becomes an expected pleasure. This form of emotional dependence is agreeable and harmless. It's pointless to create guilt over eating chocolate. Guilt detracts from the positive contribution

which pleasure gives to health. Indulging oneself with chocolate reduces stress and helps people to relax. The beneficial effect of pleasure is under-estimated (both in society and in science). Chocolate is not fattening. Chocolate is quickly digested (30 minutes), it contains theobromine, which is a true tonic, and produces endorphins which create a feeling of well-being. Because we probably only live once, these are reasons enough to eat chocolate daily, in moderation!

### A memory concerning chocolate?

Emotional dependence is a pleasure which develops during childhood. At home, there was a terracotta teapot in the cupboard near the kitchen. This is the teapot that my mother used for making hot chocolate, to give the children a treat on special occasions. Pure powdered cacao, sugar, and boiling whole milk made a chocolate drink which warmed us through and through and which created family contentment. This hot chocolate developed in us a life-long love of chocolate.

### A favourite chocolate baton?

From hot chocolate to a piece of chocolate is only a step for children. The chocolate baton is the ultimate chocolate pleasure. The baton feels really large in the child's hand. As you grow, the batons seem smaller and the pleasure is briefer. Or is that just my impression?

### Your three best pralines?

My preference is for natural flavours. Our taste buds recognise sweetness, acidity, salt and bitterness. But that's not all: the experience in the mouth is divided into firm and yielding elements. Firm like the effect of strong tea, vinegar, or wholemeal bread; yielding like fresh cream, sugar, and all refined foods. I prefer pralines which combine these two effects. The pleasure can be further enhanced by combining soft and crisp elements. Coated pralines filled with ganache retain their flavour the longest in the mouth. The higher the proportion of cocoa solids, the more bitter the ganache and the more intense is the sensation of lasting flavour

on the tongue. The praline with its ganache covered with chocolate can be a surprise, with an unexpected flavour of cinnamon, liquorice, ginger or bergamot. These are the "great vintages" from chocolate manufacturers such as Wittamer, Pierre Marcoline De Baere (in Brussels) and Del Rey (Antwerp). These pralines with their exquisite style and heady flavours are kept for special moments. They can only be eaten in very small quantities, for the point of saturation is quickly reached... This craftsman-made chocolate at the end of a meal reaches the peak of all our gastronomic desires, like a glass of port. There is also the memory, happy and contented, of what has been eaten, while enjoying privileged moments to come ...

JO GRYN, OR "CHAMBERTIN" (EDITOR IN CHIEF, *THE GAULT-MILLAU BELGIUM* GUIDE AND GASTRONOMIC REPORTER ON THE DAILY PAPER *LE SOIR*)

### A passion for chocolate?

You dream of it when you are still a tiny child, when you are old enough to drink it, lick it, break it, then to sneak it out of the cupboard where your parents hide it. You get up in the night to delight in it, like the fads of a pregnant woman. You think you have passed the age to appreciate it, you find it waiting faithfully on your pillow in large hotels, you are driven mad by the range of varieties developed by our chocolate and praline manufacturers. Like those bits of sticking plaster which clung to Stan Laurel's fingers, you can't get away from it. There is always someone kind enough to offer you a carton full of pralines. This is the delicate moment of choice, when parents have the chance of protecting themselves from the taste of children who ignore the liqueur pralines ... Later, in the restaurant, chocolate - the only true gastronomic substance which is black - invades our plates at the end of the meal. It is the caviar of desserts, the one that we never tire of.

### A memory concerning chocolate?

Childhood memories take two forms. First, the powder which I loved to add to a well-buttered piece of bread so that it clung on well, so as not to lose a single grain on its way to my mouth. The other memory comes from the collection of coloured prints which were found in Jacques chocolate wrappers. How did we get hold of the albums? It's terrible, I can't remember. And then, why did I give up the Jacques pictures one day and go over to Côte d'Or's Artis points? I've forgotten. If chocolate is good for the memory, I obviously didn't eat enough when I was a boy! But it was a luxury, after all, we didn't have it every day ...

### A favourite chocolate baton? Your three best pralines?

... That childhood frustration has I think left with me with an unreasonable passion for chocolate, all batons and pralines together!

SAÂD KETTANI
(GASTRONOMIC REPORTER FOR THE
MAGAZINE NATURE ET EVASION)

### A passion for chocolate?

A passion for chocolate? Not at all! - an absolute vice! White, milk, filled, fondant ... For every taste and any time of the day. And it's a passion that can't be explained. But good chocolate - like a good wine - deserves the best. A dark chocolate, 70 per cent pure, compared to a milk chocolate which is too rich and too sugary, can be compared to a fine Madiran wine compared to a rosé wine from Anjou. The image is a bit cheeky - but connoisseurs will understand. What is simple is not necessarily better!

### A memory related to chocolate?

As far back as I can remember, one of my most moving gourmet memories is connected to chocolate. A baton of (good) chocolate simply slipped into a piece of (good) bread which I ate at tea-time during my summer holidays. A bitter-sweet recollection ...

### A favourite chocolate baton?

For me the passion for chocolate is particularly linked to fondant. A plain chocolate without artifice, to break in the hand. The Côte d'Or dark is what I expect of a chocolate. For more subtle pleasures I turn instead to a craftsman's coating chocolate which I cut into with a chopping knife (I find that splinters of chocolate have something attractively wild and authentic about them) and which I consume with a glass of Maury wine (preferably from Mas Amiel).

### Your three best pralines?

I am not a great praline addict! However, my inclination towards baroque flavours takes me to combinations of flavours which are sometimes strange. I adore the sacred mixture of orange and chocolate to be found in orangettes. Another real love: lemon or Earl Grey tea ganache (from the Mont Royal chocolate facto-

ry at Uccle, for example). These dark chocolate pralines (as bitter as you like) are filled with a wonderfully smooth cream.

MAIRE-JO DENISTY
("COOKERY" SECTION IN *FEMMES-D'AUJOURD'HUI*)

### A passion for chocolate?

If the world strikes us as sad without the scent of jam (said Georges Duhamel), it would be sadder still without the aroma of chocolate ... Can you imagine birthdays and celebrations without chocolate? Easter without chocolate Easter eggs? Christmas without pralines? When a feast is being prepared it takes over the house, for without it there are no desserts worthy of the name. They may be called profiteroles, merveilleux, marquises, javanais, éclairs, mousses ... and bring a gleam to the eye of the well-fed guest. The first cake that all little girls dream of making is always a chocolate cake.

### A memory concerning chocolate?

Throughout my early childhood, chocolate was a mythical and unknown food, people talked about it, about how they `used to eat it'. That was during the last war. And then I discovered it, at the Liberation. Like all children then, no doubt I ate it without moderation at first ...

### A favourite chocolate baton?

I like to break into chocolate batons with whole hazelnuts. The smoothness of the chocolate, the crack of the nuts, make a harmonious and balanced whole. But a very dark and very bitter chocolate is always welcome with the little cup of expresso coffee late in the morning.

### Your three best pralines?

My choice of pralines? `Bonaparte' from Neuhaus, with their shape which vaguely recalls the famous hat, with its delicious coffee flavour, the `Astrid' dusted with sugar which melts on the tongue when the veil of sugar has cracked, from the same manufacturer, and the `orangettes', where the blend of preserved orange peel and dark chocolate is highly successful. ...

# And because everyth

Of course, there used to be Footit and Chocolat, the two clowns of the late nineteenth century; in the music-hall there is Raymond Devos who talks about a dozen chocolate éclairs in Le Mille-Feuille. There are some films which refer to chocolate, sometimes with different meanings, like Bread and Chocolate, an Italian film from 1973, or Chocolat, with Isaac de Bankolé, a French film from 1988, or more recently Fraise et chocolat ... But it is in song that it appears most often.

In 1952, Charles Trenet gave indirect homage to the Neuhaus pharmaceutical confectioners in his song as he returned from Quebec - the beginning of Dans les pharmacies runs, "Dans les pharmacies, dans les pharmacies/On vend du nougat et du chocolat ..." ("In the pharmacy, in the pharmacy/Nougat is sold, and chocolate too ...")

The following year, Annie Cordy (who was to return to it in 1985 with Chokakao) honoured cinema usherette/sales assistants and their famous interval trays, in the song for the film Boum sur Paris : "Sweets, toffees..." which whole cinema audiences took up as a refrain: "... ices, chocolates..."

In the same way, François Chalais narrates his memoirs under the title Les Chocolats de l'entracte ("The Interval Chocolates") and the talented cinema critic on the Paris daily paper Le Soir, Luc Honorez, imagined in L'Ouvreuse aux bas de soie ("The usherette in silk stockings") a "chocolate ice-cream murder", worthy of the Marquis de Sade!

In the 1960s, Joe Dassin sang Le Petit Pain au chocolat. In 1966 Bobby Lapointe began his most famous song,

# ...ng ends with a song...

Aragon et Castille, *with these words: "I prefer chocolate ice creams..."*

*Pierre Perret referred to it - knowing that it was discovered in Mexico - in* Tonton Cristobal *(1967): "The morning after chocolate you make believe/and spit out like they do in Mexico ..."*

*In 1974, because it was a story of childhood, it was not surprising that the word appeared in Alain Souchon's* Dix Ans: *"On Wednesdays I go for a walk/with a straw in my lemonade/I'm going to annoy the vanilla pegs/and the chocolate lads..."*

*In 1980, Salvatore Adamo published a collection of poems,* Le Charmeur d'océans, *in which* Jemappes sur hier *evokes an episode in his childhood: "And avoiding paying for my ticket for the flicks/and pinching chocolate to impress the gang/which I took back next day/without the shopkeeper knowing/and who didn't expect as much ..."*

*We have a traditional lullaby written in the nineteenth century, sung to an 18th-century tune and no doubt still sung today,* Fais dodo, *("Go to sleep"): "Go to sleep, Colas my little brother/go to sleep, you will have some cash/Maman is upstairs/making us cake/Papa is downstairs/making chocolate ..."*

*To finish this guide with a children's lullaby seems symbolic, and an ideal way to remember that chocolate awakens the element of childhood which is in all of us, reviving the feelings and the innocence of pleasure ...*

# Glossary

(In many cases, French terms are retained in the English vocabulary of chocolate.)

*Alcaloid:* Basic nitrogenous organic compound of vegetable origin. Example: morphine, quinine, etc.

*Amber:* flavour or colour of grey amber (intestinal concretion from sperm whales).

*Brisure:* crisp flake or broken fragment

*Broyage:* crushing into tiny pieces by pressure or blows

*Candy-bar:* Confectionery bar, generic English name used for filled and chocolate-covered bars (such as "Mars")

*Cantharides:* a golden-green insect (coleoptera), 2 cm long, common on ash-trees. In powdered form, they were used in aphrodisiac preparations

*Cerisette:* chocolate with dried cherry

*Cerneau:* the heart, or kernel, of a green walnut

*Chantilly or crème Chantilly or whipped cream:* fresh cream thoroughly emulsified and sweetened

*Concassage:* crushing, chopping or chopping up into fragments of greater or smaller size

*Conchage:* conching, making the cocoa paste more fluid by blending in cocoa butter

*Copeau:* a chip or flake sliced off a block with a sharp blade

*Cuvette:* chocolate formed into a small cup, to act as the base for a praline and designed to contain a filling such as marzipan

*Dresser:* to build up or present

*Emonder:* to blanch or strip off the skin (of almonds, for example)

*Fourrage:* the inner filling of a praline

*Franchise:* a shop with the right to use a brand or company name under certain conditions

*Glucose:* sweet-tasting glucid found in certain fruits, such as grapes, and used for preparing almost all glucids

*Kirsch:* brandy made with fermented cherries or wild cherries

*Marble:* the marble sheet or table on which the craftsman chocolate-maker pours liquid chocolate to work with it

*Napper:* to cover with a liquid thickened to coating consistency

*Pommader:* creaming, to soften butter with a whisk to a spreading consistency

*Snack:* the English word is a generally recognised term for a small item of food, not part of a meal

*Tempering:* preparing the chocolate in a special machine, melting it to more than 50° and cooling it gradually to just over 30° to achieve the right viscosity for the moulding

*Torrefaction:* roasting the beans

*Tourteau:* "cake", the solid residue left when all oils have been extracted from nuts, etc. The "cake" derived from cocoa beans is used for cocoa powder

# Bibliography

## 1. History and general

Jean-Claude Bologne, *Histoire morale et culturelle de nos boissons*, Laffont, 1991

Jeanne Bourrin, preface, *Le Livre du chocolat*, Flammarion, 1995

Sandra Boyton, *Les Cinglés du chocolat*, Hermé, 1987

Anthelme Brillat-Savarin, *La Physiologie du goût*, Flammarion, 1973

Chantal Coady, *Chocolate, the Food of the Gods*, Pavilion, 1993

Henry Dorchy, *Le Moule à chocolat*, Editions de l'Amateur, 1987

Sylvie Girard, *Le Guide du chocolat*, Messidor, 1984

Nikita Harwich, *L'Histoire du cacao et du chocolat*, Desjonquères, 1992

Jean Heer, *Nestlé, 125 ans*, Nestlé, 1991

Claude Lebey, *Le Guide des croqueurs de chocolat*, Julliard, 1994

Robert Linxe, *La Maison du chocolat*, Laffont, 1992

Jacques Mercier, *Le Chocolat belge*, Glénat, 1989

Léo Moulin, *Les Liturgies de la table*, fonds Mercator, 1990

Jill Norman, *Le Chocolat*, Laffont, 1990

Catherine de Sairigne, *Le Chocolat, le thé, le café*, Gallimard, 1984

Wolfgang Schievelbush *Histoire des stimulants,* Le Promeneur, 1991

Lutgarde Swaelen, *L'Europe à table*, Musée Bourwerhuis, Antwerp, 1993

CGER exhibition catalogue, Brussels, 1996

*Histoire des transports publics à Bruxelles*, STIB

## 2. Literature

Salvatore Adamo, *Le Charmeur d'océans*, Editions de la Lande, 1980

François Chalais, *Les Chocolats de l'entracte*, Stock, 1972

René Hénoumont, *Café liégeois*, CE, 1984

Luc Honorez, *L'Ouvreuse aux bas de soie*, Ercée, 1989

David Lodge, *Therapy,* Penguin Books, 1996

Amélie Nothomb, *Péplum*, Albin Michel, 1996

## 3. Recipes, diet

Maurice Bernachon, *La Passion du chocolat*, Flammarion, 1985

Jef Damme, *Le Chocolat*, Lannoo, 1993

Marcel Desaulniers, *Mourir de chocolat*, Minerva, 1992

Roger Geerts, *Pralines belges*, Lannoo, 1983

Martine Jolly, *Le Chocolat, une passion dévorante*, Laffont, 1983

Christian Souris, *La Folle histoire de la cuisine wallone*, Quorum, 1995

Marie-Blanche Vergne, *Les Desserts au chocolat*, Solar, 1992

# Index

ISBN 2-8046-0165-x
Printed in France by PubliPhotOffset - Pantin.
Legal deposit: october 97.